INDIA TO ETHIOPIA

INDIA TO ETHIOPIA

A 50 Year Journey

Robert Revie

RITCHIE
John Ritchie Publishing

40 Beansburn, Kilmarnock, Scotland

ISBN-13: 978 1 910513 95 8

Copyright © 2017 by John Ritchie Ltd.
40 Beansburn, Kilmarnock, Scotland

www.ritchiechristianmedia.co.uk

Typeset by John Ritchie Ltd., Kilmarnock
Printed by Bell & Bain, Glasgow

Contents

India to Ethiopia

Foreword

It gives me great pleasure to write a Foreword to this book, not least because of the special relationship that has existed between the Revie and McQuoid families since we first met in 1969 in the rural town of Batie, northern Ethiopia, when the Revie family came to join the small team of missionaries who were serving God among Muslim and 'Orthodox Christian' people.

I had the pleasure of helping Robert and Sheena with their initial *Amharic* language study, but in the middle of their course of studies, the McQuoid family (at that time two adults and two young children) had to move 250 miles to Addis Ababa, the capital city, to start a new work.

The Revie family (also two adults and two children) came with us to finish their language study course, and for several months shared our home and our lives, and were of great help at the start of our new work.

Since those early days, in our personal lives, both Robert Revie and I have experienced a deep sorrow, we have shared a common joy, and we have lived in the light of a thrilling expectation.

Our **sorrow** is that each of us lost his dearly-beloved wife (his children's mother, his companion in God's work) - Valerie McQuoid and Sheena Revie.

Our **joy** is that our children - 3 Revies and 3 McQuoids - have made wise choices in their lives, and are all true followers of Christ.

Our **expectation** - when our Lord Jesus Christ comes - is the thrill of seeing again the wife we have lost, and the Ethiopians we have, by God's grace, won for Christ.

May God bless you, Robert, and your book, and all who read it.

John McQuoid
Northern Ireland
September 2017

Acknowledgements

I am grateful to my family who have given much help and advice which I have deeply appreciated.

I am grateful to Bert Cargill for his meticulous work in editing this book and giving advice where necessary.

I have appreciated a long association with my dear colleague John McQuoid both in Ethiopia and here in this country. John has very willingly agreed to write the Foreword. I first came to know John at Batie when he was our language teacher and that friendship has deepened over the years.

I appreciate the help that Stewart Rollo has given in producing a very fine cover for the book and although we gave him a hard time initially, Stewart finally did an excellent job.

I am indebted to the publisher, John Ritchie Ltd, for all the input they have provided and also for their help in advertising the book. Their support in different ways has meant so much to me.

I am also deeply thankful to all who over 50 years have prayed privately and collectively for the work of God we have been involved in both in Ethiopia and in the UK. Without your support of intercession that work would never have been achieved. Many will see and read of what God has done in Ethiopia and will be aware that God has answered prayer.

I am grateful for those who have showed their support in the work of the Lord by supporting us practically and Sheena and I were often speechless when that practical support was given. Much of that support has been channelled into the work of God in Ethiopia and in a coming day many from Ethiopia will thank God for what has been accomplished through your kindness.

It is my desire that through the reading of the book many will begin to show a deeper interest in Ethiopia. I pray that it will encourage them to pray regularly for this needy country. Any profits from the sale of this book will be ploughed back into the work in Ethiopia.

Introduction

This short book has been written to record some of the many experiences Sheena and I have encountered over 50 years in Ethiopia and also in Scotland.

Although we felt that we were going to be in Ethiopia for a lifetime that came to an abrupt halt in 1978. Because of the introduction of communism in 1974 we were unable to continue to serve God in Ethiopia and we left in 1978. We were out of the country for 15 years but we were able to return in 1993.

Since that time God has done a remarkable work in Ethiopia, and many believers said that they felt that our experience during the past 20 years should be put in print. This book is the result.

It has been a real privilege to serve God in the country that received the Gospel initially by the Ethiopian eunuch and it has been thrilling to see so many who have trusted in Christ.

What has impressed me is the way that our Ethiopian evangelists have reached out to new areas with the Gospel. What a thrill to see so many who have been delivered from Satan worship and idolatry trust in Christ.

New areas are being reached each year and it has been wonderful to see God at work in these areas.

Robert Revie
Tarbolton
Scotland
November 2017

CHAPTER ONE

Family History

In July 1967 Robert and Sheena Revie were ready to embark on a completely new Christian ministry in India. They had sold their modest home in Armadale, distributed their furniture, and had sent all their goods to Southampton to be forwarded to India by ship. Robert had left his job as a medical sales representative and the last fortnight was to be spent at Sheena's parents' home. They had said goodbye to their many friends on 18th June 1967 at a commending meeting held in Armadale town hall.

Twelve days before their sailing date they received a telephone call from the Indian Embassy in London to say that they could not proceed to India as a new law had been passed in parliament refusing missionary nurses entry to India. The Revies were deeply saddened but the events that followed must be kept till later in this enthralling story.

This is my story which began on 19th April 1937. It was when I became part of the Revie family in a place called Byres Road, in Partick, a suburb in the west of Glasgow. But let me go further back, as far back as I have been told, to relate how the story of the Revie family began to unfold. For this history I can go back only three generations.

My paternal great grandparents lived in Tarbert on the Kintyre Peninsula where Joseph Revie, my great grandfather worked as the local blacksmith. They had 10 children within the space of 14 years with three infant deaths that was more or less a commonplace family situation in the 19th century. Joseph was a church elder and an ardent supporter of the temperance movement and my grandfather was the youngest of this large family. Someone wrote in a biographical article, 'A knowledge of our forebears is highly important if we are to understand ourselves and give of our best in the society in which we find answers. We can observe their characteristics in our *behaviour. We can learn from their failures, both moral and physical and of course from their successes'.*

A tragedy struck the Kintyre Peninsula in 1873. A small boy arrived in Tarbert for an indefinite holiday with relatives, and as he lived close to the smithy he often visited it to watch the work in progress. When two days passed with no daily call, Joseph my great grandfather made enquiries as to the reason for the boy's absence.

The little lad was dangerously ill with a fever and his life seemed to be in danger. Joseph spent one night's vigil in the small sick room to relieve the exhausted relatives. Doubtless he was relieved to learn a short time later that the little boy had passed the crisis and was making a slow recovery.

**Joseph & Martha Revie
with infant Mary
1860**

Alas, too late it was discovered that the illness was the dreaded smallpox and the Revie family were stricken with the disease after a few days. Joseph became unwell and after a week of illness he died on 14th November 1873 being only 43.

Martha his wife wrote to her brother and sister, '*Dear brother and sister, it is with deep sorrow that I have to let you know of the death of my dear husband who died this day at 2pm after a short illness*'. The death certificate was signed by his nephew Robert Sliman but sadly 10 days later he also died just 26 years of age.

On 28th November, Joseph's wife Martha aged 38 also died of the disease. The oldest daughter Mary aged 14 had been caring for her mother and she had gone to the outer pump to get some cold water, but when she returned she found her mother had passed away. Helen aged 8 was the third victim and she died on 30th November after an illness of seven days.

At this point the death toll ceased, but the infection is said to have spread through the entire family, and following their mother's death Mary and the younger members of the family were locked in an isolation ward.

They were left with no nursing care at all and they were expected to look after themselves. At intervals a jug of gruel and a few slices of bread were pushed in through the window and the window was then shut. At this time Duncan was 12, Joseph was 6, Martha was 4, Archibald was 3, and William, my grandfather, was 18 months old.

Sixty five years later, Duncan Revie, the second oldest, who then lived in New Zealand related the story of these sad days. He said he would never forget Mary burning with fever climbing through the window to a nearby well head pump. She pumped and pumped the water relieving her burning thirst and cooling her fevered body and that was what saved her life.

With the abatement of the fever, returning strength brought severe hunger pains. Mary plotted with Duncan that when it was dark they would climb out of the window and return to their home at the smithy. The little band climbed over a stone wall into a field of turnips and they began to eat the frozen roots of the turnips to stave off the hunger pains.

When eventually they reached home they were deeply shocked to discover it was completely deserted and locked securely, a plague-house indeed. Belatedly news was sent to their mother's sister who came in her horse-drawn carriage and subsequently took the children back to her home. Mercifully they all survived and when the time came for them to be cared for they were split up and sent to different family members to be cared for. My father only knew his own father and an uncle who later became Dr Archie Revie in Kilmarnock.

My grandfather had been brought up by his aunt Mary in the fear of the Lord but like Cornelius of Acts 10 he needed to have an experience of new birth. He attended services conducted by the well-known evangelist D.L. Moody, but although he was impressed by the Gospel messages he did not at that time trust the Saviour. Shortly after his marriage, he attended meetings conducted by John McNeil, a well-known evangelist, and one night when the preacher told the story in John chapter 9 of the man who was born blind, he looked up to the gallery where my grandfather was sitting and cried, 'Young man, receive your sight.' This was the moment when my grandfather was saved.

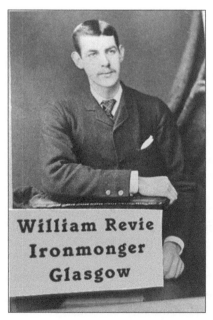

One night in Glasgow, my grandparents stood listening to a company preaching in the open air and when the invitation was given to join them they followed the group into Abingdon Hall in Partick, and soon they were baptised and received into their fellowship. From his earliest Christian life, my grandfather had a great interest in working among children and teenagers and that interest never wavered through his whole life.

My grandfather, William Revie, tragically died in the 'flu epidemic of 1919 leaving three boys - Joseph, Neil and Craig, and one girl Martha, all relatively young with my father Craig being only 16 years old.

The year 1919 seemed to be etched on my father's mind. The 'flu epidemic was sweeping the country and with no antibiotics then, many were taken suddenly. During this year my grandfather became quite ill and in a very short time he was called home to heaven.

For some time, the family lived at Kirn near Dunoon. At that time, they found it difficult to make ends meet and after some business ventures that didn't seem to succeed, the family moved to Glasgow.

Before the sad event of his father's death, my father began to be troubled about his own soul and after having a long conversation with his father he trusted the Saviour. Later he was baptised and received into the assembly at Shiloh Hall in the district of Shettleston on the east side of Glasgow.

My maternal grandparents were Robert and Agnes Crawford and around 1918 my grandfather trained as a butcher and set up a butcher's business in Shettleston and they were in the Shiloh Hall assembly. They had four children, Mary who was my mother, Leila, Ewing and James, and during that time my father became friendly with the Crawford family.

Not too long afterwards the Crawford's moved to Stronardron farm in Glendaruel to manage a sheep farm and my father and his brothers moved to Kirn near Dunoon around the same time.

It was during this time that my father made acquaintance with my mother and when he visited Glendaruel my grandmother welcomed him - but made sure that he did not outstay his welcome!

Around 1928 the Crawfords moved to a farm near Newton Mearns called North Moorhouse, and their daughter Leila commenced training as a nurse in Glasgow Royal Infirmary with a view to serving God as a missionary in Brazil. I remember spending many happy school holidays at the farm. It was at the farm that my parents were married in 1932 and they then set up home in an area of Glasgow called Ibrox.

My grandfather Crawford like my grandfather Revie was also extremely capable at teaching the Bible to children. I remember my father telling me about the night my grandfather spoke on the lost sheep in Luke chapter 15.

He had one of the boys crossing the platform carrying the little lamb that had been lost and then was found by the shepherd. The young boy carrying the lamb happened to be Willie Maxwell who later married Leila Crawford and they went as missionaries to Brazil to serve the Lord there for a lifetime.

When my parents set up home in Ibrox, their next door neighbours were a Mr and Mrs Stewart who had come from the north east of Scotland and both couples were in an assembly called Plantation St for about two years. Plantation St assembly ultimately moved to Harley St in Ibrox a number of years later.

My parents then moved to Partick and after a short time the family moved to Hillington where I grew up till teenage years. My family consisted of Nan who was born in 1933, Willie in 1934, myself in 1937, Margaret in 1939 and Neil in 1948.

I attended Hillington Primary School and then I continued my secondary education at Bellahouston Academy. I remember as a child the nightly raids of German planes trying to bomb the Rolls Royce factory which was only about 2 miles from our home and at that time it was producing the Spitfire engines. The factory's roof had been covered by grass and it was never hit.

The air raid siren in our area was situated in the Hillington Primary School, which I attended later, and whenever the siren went off everyone ran for the Anderson shelters situated in each garden.

My mother often kept us in the house and we crouched behind a large sofa where she would read to us either a story from the Bible or at other times a story from Aesop's Fables. This was to keep our minds from what was happening outside. We would often ask mother to read louder to block out the noise of the bombs being dropped near us, shattering many of the windows.

As the situation deteriorated, my grandfather suggested that we move to the farm near Newton Mearns where he felt it would be safer and during this time, at the age of four, I attended the Newton Mearns Primary School. After about two years, when things were a bit quieter, we returned to Hillington.

My parents were believers as were my grandparents on both sides, and my parents worshipped at Halfway Gospel Hall, Cardonald which had recently commenced and I attended this hall on a regular basis.

The war ended in May 1945 and I remember passing the paper shop and seeing the huge headline on the newspaper 'Peace at last'. That headline was one I kept thinking about for some time and on the 21st October 1945 after hearing a very solemn message on the coming of the Lord, at the age of 8, I went home and kneeling at my bedside with my father beside me I trusted the Saviour.

I remember writing to my grandfather to tell him I had trusted in Christ as my Saviour and he sent me a lovely reply and in it he had an acrostic written of the word 'Jesus'. It was Jesus - Eternally - Saves - Us - Sinners. He then suggested that I try and make another acrostic with the same word Jesus. I remember how I treasured that letter and kept it in my wallet for many years.

In 1952, the Crawfords sold their farm at North Moorhouse near Newton Mearns and they moved to Prestwick. At about the same time, my Uncle Ewing and Aunt Jean moved to Prestwick, and bought a dairy, delivering milk in Prestwick.

At this time I had become a bit tired of school, especially algebra and trigonometry in mathematics and I decided to leave school at the age of 16 having completed my O grades. I then went to stay with my Uncle Ewing who had the dairy business in Prestwick.

During the next two years, as well as helping to deliver the milk daily (apart from Christmas Day) I worked in Burtons the tailors in Ayr. My Uncle Ewing had a pony and a wooden trailer. I would begin work at about 5am delivering the milk, but that was not easy in winter time.

My grandfather used to help me on the milk run at that time. Sadly, in July 1956, he had a stroke while painting a wall at the dairy. He was rushed to hospital and died a week later.

My family moved to Prestwick in 1954 and we all worshipped at Glenburn Gospel Hall.

Revie family 1954

CHAPTER TWO
Spiritual Development

It was when I went to Prestwick that I began to think seriously about spiritual matters. I was baptised at the age of 16 in Bute Hall, Prestwick as there was no baptismal tank in the old hall at Glenburn, and I was received into fellowship in Glenburn Gospel Hall.

The assembly in Glenburn was an excellent training ground where many opportunities were given to serve the Lord. I soon became a Sunday School teacher and many years later I received a letter from one of my Sunday School pupils who had gone on to live for God in another country.

When one reads the Bible, it often portrays family traits both good and bad being passed on to the next generation. If you consider the life of Abraham he lied twice about Sarah being his sister and not his wife and so did Isaac lie about Rebekah. When you consider the life of Isaac and Rebekah there was partiality in the family towards their two boys and this was also repeated in Jacob's family.

As I reflected in later life, I remembered that both my grandfathers were very gifted in speaking to children, as was my father. With that kind of family background I followed in their footsteps and was involved in children's and youth ministry for much of my life. Only eternity will reveal the results of the seed that was sown over these many years in this ministry. I would always encourage those who were younger to get involved in the ministry of work among children.

There were many opportunities for preaching the Gospel and I remember the first time I preached at the Gospel Hall in Glenburn. I shared the service with John Currie and Robert Rae and I felt I had enough material to preach for at least half an hour. However, after about ten minutes I finished my message and felt that I would never speak again!

However, the brethren in Glenburn were so encouraging and soon I was travelling to different parts of Ayrshire with John McCloy, who later became my brother-in-law, to help where there was a small assembly. I remember at that time visiting Dailly, Crosshill, Sanquhar and Kirkconnel among other places and sharing in the preaching of the Gospel.

After my father retired from the Clyde Cold Store where he had spent all his working life, my parents lived in various places - at Elie, Dunfermline, Perth and finally Leven where my father passed away in December 1988. My mother's sister Leila Maxwell died on the same day in Brazil.

When my mother was 89 and the subject came up about her perhaps going into Auchlochan Care Home, she said that Auchlochan was just for old people! However, at the age of 91 she decided that she would go into Auchlochan for two weeks' respite care. After her respite care she decided that she wanted to go there to stay as she said she had so many visitors during her two weeks, and what she was missing most in life was company. She then spent two very happy years in Auchlochan and had many visitors. She lived next door to Mrs Stewart who with her husband had commenced their married lives as their next door neighbours in Ibrox.

Mother at 92 with Betty Burnett

My mother took ill at the age of 93 and when she was leaving to go to Hospital, she thanked her carers for all their kindness. After a very short illness she went home to be with her Lord after serving Him for 80 years, having trusted the Lord as a girl of 13. I remember the day before my mother died she reminded us that it had been 11 years on the following day when my father had died. She said she would just take a long sleep and waken up in heaven and that is exactly what she did. We were so privileged to see a dear saint of God so serenely going home to heaven in this way.

My mother told me the day before she died that she and my father had prayed that one of their children would serve the Lord as a missionary. I felt that this was so sacrificial of my mother to say this as her younger sister Leila and her youngest brother James had gone to Brazil as missionaries, leaving my mother and her younger brother Ewing at home. Uncle Ewing died at the early age of 46. In spite of being denied the company of her brothers and sister for many years, she was willing for one of her own children to serve God on the mission field.

Mother also said at that time that she had prayed for her children that they might put their trust in the Lord Jesus and she had the joy of seeing that happen. She then said that she was praying for her 16 grandchildren that they too would come to know the Saviour. Then she said to us that it was now our responsibility to pray for the next generation.

Sheena and I have been very much aware of this and we have prayed for our children and grandchildren that they all might come to trust in the Saviour. We have been so aware that salvation does not 'run in the blood' and everyone must make up their own minds which road they will decide to take. We have seen grandchildren taking a different course in their lives than we would desire, but our prayer has always been that they might see the error of their ways and come to know Jesus Christ as their Saviour.

Now that Sheena is at home in heaven, I am continuing to remember the whole family in my prayers that ultimately they will all come to know the Lord Jesus as Saviour for without Him there is no hope of being in heaven.

I was associated with a family who were involved in missionary service as my aunt Leila Crawford married William Maxwell and they served God in Brazil from 1938 for the rest of their lives. My uncle James Crawford married Jenny Alan and they also went as missionaries to Brazil in 1952. In a similar way, they have devoted the rest of their lives in missionary service in Brazil and my Uncle James at the age of ninety three is still involved in preaching in Brazil.

I can clearly remember the time that my Uncle Willie and Aunt Leila with their two children Anna and Janneta came home from Brazil in 1946 after having spent 8 years there. The reason for their long stay in Brazil was the fact that the Second World War had prevented them from returning home.

We tried to communicate with Anna and Janneta, but all they knew was Portuguese as that was what they had learned while their parents were in Brazil, and Scotland to them was a foreign country.

My recollection of these days was of attending welcome home services and farewell services when a lot of tears were shed. I realised at that time the great sacrifice that was involved in this kind of service as children were separated from their parents and parents from their children and grandchildren.

I vividly remember travelling to Glasgow Central station with my family when my Uncle Willie Maxwell and Aunt Leila were leaving for Brazil. I also remember this being repeated when my Uncle James Crawford and my Aunt Jenny were leaving for Brazil. I remember as a youngster my grandfather, who had a very strong voice, leading the large number of believers in the hymn 'God be with you till we meet again'.

I remembered as a teenager thinking that serving God as a missionary was not an easy path to take as there was much sacrifice involved, not only at the beginning but right through life as many new experiences would cross our paths. There was the leaving home and family, the education of the children, concern for ageing parents, perhaps an illness in the family and so many other things that possibly you hadn't thought about when you felt that God was calling you to serve Him in this way. Having said that, there are so many incidents that bring such joy that you might never have experienced had you never embarked in this kind of service.

As we have travelled widely in Ethiopia we have become friendly with many

Ethiopians. We have also been able to see where the evangelists serve and to hear of some of the difficulties that they face in a rural community. Some have problems of the main market being convened on a Sunday. As a visit to the market is vital for the believers, they often wonder what to do. Should they have their service early on in the morning or should they go to the market and then have their service later on? These and other problems we have been able to study together.

At the judgment seat of Christ what a thrill awaits those who have been called to this service, and to see the many who have come to trust in Christ as a result of this kind of ministry. As Paul puts it in 1 Thessalonians 2:19:

'**For what is our hope, or joy, or crown of rejoicing? Are not even ye in the presence of our Lord Jesus Christ at his coming? For ye are our glory and joy.**'

CHAPTER THREE
Nursing Preparation

At this time I began to seek God's mind as far as my life was concerned. I sought the Lord's guidance as to how I should serve Him as I did not want just to drift through life as a believer without any clear direction as to what God wanted me to do. I often heard preachers saying 'Only one life, 'twill soon be past and only what's done for Christ will last'.

I felt as a result of some incidents in my life that God was calling me to be a missionary in India. I had been corresponding with Miss Jean Thomson and a Miss Isa Japp who had both spent a lifetime in India at a place called Sankeshwar. I also spoke to them both at a missionary conference in Ayr.

I felt that if God was calling me to serve Him as a missionary I should have some kind of qualification that might be beneficial in this kind of service, and as a result I decided to apply to Ballochmyle Hospital to become a qualified nurse.

I was given an appointment to see the matron on 9th August 1955. At the interview she told me that I would be accepted to train as a qualified nurse and I could commence work at the hospital on 1st November.

However, on the 25th October I was called up for National Service and I decided to register as a conscientious objector. Most of the other young men in Glenburn Gospel Hall were miners so they were exempt from National Service so I had no guidance from that quarter. However, I decided to go to the military tribunal alone. Before I went I prayed that if God wanted me to become a qualified nurse at Ballochmyle hospital and subsequently to serve God as a missionary then I would be given complete exemption from National Service.

At that time you either were refused conscientious objector status and were sent to prison, or you were given conditional exemption when you might be sent to a market garden or you might be sent to a hospital as an auxiliary, or you may be given complete exemption.

I went in fear and trembling as these judges looked so severe. At the tribunal they asked me some very difficult questions. They asked me that if a burglar had come into my home and attacked my mother - what would I do? I replied that I would, to the best of my ability, try and defend my mother from harm as that was the natural thing to do.

They then asked me that when Paul was in prison (in Acts 23) was he right to ask help and protection from the chief captain against a band of men who were intent in killing him? I said I felt that what Paul was doing was asking protection from unscrupulous men who could bring no case against him.

I wondered if my answers had satisfied the judges. Out of over 330 men who registered as conscientious objectors that year only 2 were given complete exemption and I was one of them. I was then convinced that God was leading me in a path that was His desire for my life.

Since that time I have often thought about the sovereign hand of God in my life. I thought about Paul in Acts 16 when he had purposed to go north into Phrygia and Galatia in Asia Minor where he could have spent a profitable time preaching the Gospel, but the Holy Spirit prevented him from going there. He then thought of going into Mysia for the same purpose but again he was prevented by the Spirit so he passed Mysia by and travelled on to Troas. After Paul received a night vision he travelled into Europe - a visit which might never have happened. This new move ultimately brought the message of the Gospel to the rest of Europe and eventually to the United Kingdom.

Had I been happy in school I might have gone on to higher education and would possibly have stayed in and around Glasgow. I believe that the Crawfords would have continued in farming if one of their sons had been willing to carry on in the farm, but with James going to Brazil and Ewing having already left the farm, they decided to sell the farm and move to Prestwick.

As a result of my grandparents' move I also moved down to Ayrshire and had I not been employed in Ballochmyle Hospital I might never have met Sheena. If I had not been given complete exemption on 25th October 1955 I could not have commenced in nursing in November of 1955: **'God's ways are past finding out'.**

I began at the Preliminary Training School of Nursing in January 1956 with 17 young women, I being the only male so I had quite a choice! However only four of the young women were believers so that reduced the choices! The four young women all attended Gospel Halls in different parts of Ayrshire but soon over the next six months I was drawn to one of these young women - that was Sheena Paton who came from Tarbolton. I often spoke of her as the **'bonnie lass of Ballochmyle'.**

Sheena was an only child whose parents Bill and Jean Paton attended the Gospel Hall in Tarbolton. Sheena went to the local primary school and then to the junior secondary school after which she was employed in the Co-operative in Mossblown near Annbank. As a teenager Sheena was becoming interested in local life. She was very keen on tennis and met regularly with the other teenagers in the village.

When Sheena was about 15, a series of Gospel meetings were being held in a tent in Annbank, the neighbouring village to Tarbolton. On one of the Sundays, one of the evangelists, Jim Hutchison attended the morning service in Tarbolton. On the way to Sheena's parents' home for lunch, he invited Sheena to attend the evening service in the tent and Sheena agreed to go. However, in the evening Sheena said to her father that she was going out for a walk with some of her teenage friends. When he heard this he told her that she had promised the evangelist that she would go to the tent, and rather reluctantly she agreed to attend the service.

That night as the message of the Gospel was delivered Sheena decided that she would give her life to the Lord Jesus and that decision totally changed the course of her life. After some time Sheena felt that God was calling her to serve Him as a missionary and she also decided to apply to become a nurse in Ballochmyle Hospital.

Sheena, Anne McCreadie, Jean Hunter

After about 7 months in the Training School, I was very attracted to this blonde rosy-cheeked nurse. So I said I wanted to go out with her. Sheena told me that before this could happen she would have to get permission from her parents. One evening when she returned from home she told me that her parents had given their permission and I wrote in my diary that day **'this is a red letter date in my life'.**

Early on in our courtship Sheena told me that there might be a problem in our relationship. When I asked her what the problem might be she said that God had called her to Ballochmyle Hospital to serve Him as a missionary.

I was delighted at this news as I had felt that God was also calling me to the mission field. However Sheena said that perhaps the country that I had been called to may have been a different country from the one she had been called to.

She then suggested that each of us write on a piece of paper the country to which we had been called. When the papers were exchanged there was just one country on both papers which was **India!** Sheena then came to the conclusion that God had brought us together.

Ballochmyle Hospital was a wonderful training ground and a large Nurses' Christian Fellowship was formed. Out of this Sheena and I became part of what became known as the **Ballochmyle seven**. Seven of these nurses around that time were called to serve the Lord as missionaries in various countries.

David Smith was called to serve the Lord in Borneo and he was followed by Boyd and Blanch Aitken who also went to Borneo and finally to Hong Kong. Anne McCreadie married Peter Levett and they served the Lord in Colombia. Ruth Dewhurst went to Zambia, and Sheena and I went to Ethiopia.

After some time Sheena and I were engaged but we lived in an era when we had to finish all our training before we could contemplate marriage. After qualifying as a general nurse I went to London to do a course in tropical diseases. I got a post in a hospital in Maidenhead as a theatre charge nurse and some time afterwards was promoted to a theatre superintendent.

Sheena at the same time went to Irvine Central Hospital to do midwifery. I remember the night I left on the overnight sleeper. When my mother and Sheena came to see me off there were tears shed and I felt the pain of parting, for in those days London seemed to be a far off city.

Nurses' graduation day

When we were at Ballochmyle Hospital, an approach was made to the matron to have a Nurses' Christian Fellowship. It almost seemed to an onlooker that when a person went to do their nurse training they seemed to engage in all kinds of sinful things. Many of our colleagues were heavy smokers in spite of the warnings that were being given about smoking, others were also heavy drinkers.

A Nurses' Christian Fellowship was granted by the matron. We were arranging it so we asked many of the brethren in Ayrshire to come to the hospital to preach the Gospel. Some nights we had as many as 50-60 unsaved people present at these services. As a result of this, a number of nurses were converted, and this brought us great joy to see the Lord at work in the hospital. The senior tutor was a strong committed believer and we feel that she had a very good influence with the matron.

Similar to my 1936 Austin

CHAPTER FOUR

Maidenhead and Armadale

I arrived in Maidenhead and commenced work in St Luke's Hospital [which no longer exists] and on the Friday afternoon I went up to the sitting room where the senior staff had coffee. One sister began to chat to me as I was just new to the hospital, and I told her I was going to be off for the weekend. When I told her that I knew no one in Maidenhead, she felt that for me it would be a very miserable weekend.

However, the assembly in Maidenhead was just a few hundred yards from the hospital. I went to the Breaking of Bread on the Sunday morning and I was welcomed into their fellowship. I went back in the afternoon to the Sunday School where I had a long chat with John Dean. I was so encouraged by the warmth of the believers to this stranger from Scotland who spoke with a different accent!

The evening Gospel meeting clashed with the evening meal at the hospital, but I decided to go to the evening service. After it, I was walking back to the hospital eating an apple and perhaps feeling a bit home sick when a car drew up and a Mr and Mrs Paignton asked me where I was going.

When I said I was just returning to the hospital Mr and Mrs Paignton invited me home for supper. I had a wonderful evening with them and discovered during the evening that Mrs Paignton had worked in Muller's homes for orphans in Bristol for many years. The friendship that was formed that night continued till both Mr and Mrs Paignton were called home to heaven in their 90s.

I went on duty on Monday morning and met the same sister at the coffee break. She asked how the weekend had gone. I told her that I had a wonderful weekend! She then asked me to explain why it was so wonderful as I knew no one in Maidenhead. I told her that I went to the Gospel Hall near the hospital on the Sunday and the 80 or so believers meeting there were now my friends - and I was out for supper at one of their homes on the Sunday night.

When she heard this news, she told me she was amazed as she had been a member of the local Church of England in Maidenhead for 20 years and the only person that had shaken her hand was the local vicar. I then began to appreciate practically what fellowship in the assemblies really meant.

After I was there for a few months, I told the Paigntons that my fiancé was coming down to Maidenhead for the weekend. They said immediately that she would stay with them and they then asked her name. When I told them it was Sheena Paton they were amazed that her name was so similar to theirs.

Around this time I had bought a bicycle, but contemplating marriage in a few months I felt that some other transport was needed. After looking around for a while, I discovered a 1936 Austin 10 for sale. I decided to part with the £50 that was being asked for it.

The car had leather seats and I felt like a king as I travelled overnight to Tarbolton shortly before our marriage. I arrived at Tarbolton about 6am but felt it was a bit early to waken the Patons. After some time I was welcomed into 9 Sandgate. When Sheena asked me how I had come I told her to look out the window as I hadn't told her about buying the car.

In May 1961, Sheena and I were married in Glenburn Gospel Hall by Mr A.M.S Gooding. After our honeymoon spent in Bangor, Northern Ireland we travelled to Maidenhead in our Austin 10 with all the wedding gifts packed into the car and some loaded onto the boot which opened down to provide a handy platform for the extras.

There was a problem though! During the journey, the horn came on and would not stop, so I had to go into the first garage where a friendly mechanic unhooked it till we reached home. As there was no M6 at that time it took a long time to reach Maidenhead.

In May 1962 our first child Crawford was born in Canadian Red Cross Hospital.

Interestingly, many years later Crawford and his wife Fiona would spend about 9 years in Prince Edward Island in Canada.

After 2 years in Maidenhead, where we were in very happy fellowship at Parkside Hall, we moved to Armadale in West Lothian in Scotland. The reason for this move was that I had been accepted as a medical representative in the east of Scotland. We spent the next five years in happy fellowship with the believers in Armadale, and that was where Jane our second child was born at home in September 1964.

When we went to Armadale, I became involved in both Gospel preaching and ministry in different assemblies in the east of Scotland. I was also involved with the Bible Class in Armadale. Along with Michael Drummond I helped to run a children's meeting in a village called Blackridge nearby. I also helped in a large children's meeting in Armadale itself.

On a number of occasions when the subject of the mission field came up, Sheena being an only child said she was concerned about her parents' welfare. She felt that if she went to the mission field and they became ill, she had a responsibility for them.

However, one night when I was on business in Ireland, Sheena's mother assured her that if she and I were being called to serve the Lord as missionaries, she should not allow her parents to stand in our way as they had committed her to God's service even before she was born.

As a result, the next week I approached the brethren in Armadale about this matter. They said that they were surprised that I had not spoken to them earlier, and they very warmly commended Sheena and me to serve the Lord in India. The Armadale brethren were joined in their commendation by Glenburn, Tarbolton and Maidenhead assemblies.

A farewell meeting was held on the 18th June 1967 in the Armadale Town Hall when about 400 believers gathered to bid us farewell. We then packed all our goods and sent them to Southampton to be shipped to India. I finished work as a medical representative, we sold our house in Armadale, and as a family went through to Tarbolton to spend the last two weeks with Sheena's parents.

About 12 days before we were due to sail for India, we received a telephone call from the Indian Embassy to be told that the Indian government had changed their policy about foreign missionary nurses, and as a result we could not go to India.

Both of us were deeply saddened by this news and for a time we wondered if we had made a mistake. However we received much encouragement during this time from different believers. One brother who is now in heaven gave me a word of encouragement which I have never forgotten which was **'The streams of God cannot be stemmed, they can only be diverted'.** He reminded me, as mentioned earlier, about Paul's experience in Acts 16 and applied it to the door that had been shut for us to India.

I decided to redeem the time for the next few months so I joined a VW garage in Ayr for three months to learn some of the basics in car maintenance. This stood us in good stead as this was the kind of vehicles that were used in Ethiopia.

I also worked on a building site for a few months and helped in a variety of jobs with joiners, electricians and bricklayers. During these difficult months I was not paid for this work, but the Lord provided for us.

Sheena and I were now much in prayer as to what the Lord had in mind for us, and it seemed that God was redirecting us to another country - which was Ethiopia. This was confirmed in a number of ways. A Dr Hanton who was associated with Medical Missionary News told us that there was a need in Ethiopia for nurses and that a Mr and Mrs Bill Taylor had just gone there to help in the work of God.

We had always believed that a need did not necessarily constitute a call, so we felt that the way that God was guiding us had to be very clear for us. There were other guiding factors about Ethiopia, but both of us wanted to be doubly sure that this was the Lord's mind for us.

One day we both prayed that during that particular day someone would speak about Ethiopia in our presence. Nothing happened all day and finally, in the evening, we went to the assembly prayer meeting. During the prayer meeting, one young man got up and in his prayer he quoted part of Esther 1:1 which states **'from India to Ethiopia'**!

How one could manage to put that verse into a prayer is amazing, and Sheena and I were now sure that this was the way ahead for us. As I look back now over these 50 years, and especially after visiting India for the first time in 2017, I am convinced that the Lord made the right decision for Sheena and me to be a part of God's work in Ethiopia.

Revie family 1971

CHAPTER FIVE

Leaving and Arriving

Having had confirmed to us that God was leading us clearly to Ethiopia, Sheena and I applied for visas and we were accepted to travel to Ethiopia which we did in February 1969. A second farewell meeting was held in Tarbolton, and we left for Ethiopia from Glasgow by plane.

William Stewart, a believer from Saltcoats, had a travel agents business in Prestwick and he arranged our travel for our first journey to Ethiopia. He also helped in many subsequent travels to Ethiopia for a number of years.

After we left for Ethiopia, William and his wife Ina moved into the small assembly at Tarbolton and were a great help to that assembly for a number of years as our absence had left a gap there. It is amazing that from this small assembly two couples - Boyd and Blanch Aitken and Sheena and I - were commended and supported for over 50 years of service.

We thought that we were getting away quietly, but when we reached the airport there was a large company of believers who, when we arrived, broke into song with the words 'God be with you till we meet again'. Someone in the airport asked William if we were famous stars but he told them that we were just two nurses going to Ethiopia as Christian missionaries.

William had arranged the flight to go via Rome where we spent an overnight and the next day. There was to be an appearance of the Pope that day and we were taken by a guide to see him, but the guide also took us to the place where the apostle Paul was finally imprisoned.

We were much more interested in this visit. When we stood in the cold underground building where Paul was imprisoned for the last time, we were reminded of his words to Timothy: **'The cloak that I left at Troas with**

Carpus, when you come, bring with you, and the books, but especially the parchments'. As this was February it was extremely cold in that underground prison. Paul was a man whose life and service has had such a great impact on many believers' lives for two millennia.

We arrived in Addis Ababa where we were met by John and Martie Flynn who had been working in Ethiopia since 1952. After all the preliminaries were seen to and after Sheena and I had received our residence work permits, we travelled with them to Batie, a distance of over 400 kilometres.

John had a small Volkswagen Beetle and along with John and Martie were Sheena and I and the two children, Crawford and Jane, who were now aged six and four, all squeezed into the Beetle with some of the luggage on the roof rack.

One like John Flynn's VW beetle

The road to Batie was very rough at that time and the journey took all day. To put it mildly, we found the journey hazardous. When we arrived at Batie around 7pm, after spending the whole day travelling, we were introduced to the other missionaries who were there at that time. They were John and Valerie McQuoid and Bill and Kath Taylor and they had prepared a lovely supper for us. However, both Sheena and I did not feel like eating anything at all.

Later, we were escorted to our new home which had been built by John Flynn, helped by local workers. The house was made of a frame made of undressed wood, then filled in with bamboo and finally plastered with mud which hadn't dried out, as there had been unusually heavy rains in February that year. There was no electricity and the water had to come from the local river so it was quite an introduction to life in Ethiopia.

I felt it keenly bringing Sheena to such conditions after only 6 years of marriage, but she took everything in her stride and never complained. Of course, there were no mobile phones, and one had to go to the hotel where, after winding up the phone, you had to shout into the antiquated apparatus to get a connection.

When we got up in the mornings, all our clothes were damp and Sheena was quite sure that the children would get pneumonia, but we survived. The first word that I learned in the Amharic language was ዝናብ [rain] for when the guard came up to our house he would hold out his hand and say ዝናብ.

The only other means of communication available was to sit in front of an oil lamp and write letters to the family. Sheena's mother and my mother were so faithful in all the years we were in Ethiopia in sending letters on a very regular basis and that was greatly appreciated.

One incident that we later experienced brought home the importance of communication. News had come through that Philip, youngest son of my brother Willie, had a nasty fall at home, striking his head as the children played in the attic and he was in a serious condition in hospital. I went to the nearest town to try and find out more information and although I tried for two days to get through by telephone, it was all to no avail. It was in times like these that we felt so far away.

Sometimes we would receive a tape from home and as we listened to a familiar voice or to someone singing a lump would come to our throat and a tear come to the eye as we genuinely felt home sick.

However, we soon unpacked and got things into order although most of our goods had to be brought later from Assab, the main sea port at that time. Everything was new to us, but we soon became accustomed to the noise of the hyenas in nearby fields at night and the loud noises of the frogs in the local river bed.

The food was so different to what we had been used to. No matter where we went, we were given this large crumpet looking bread called 'Injura' which was greyish in colour and sour to taste. You then took the Injura and tore off a piece which was then dipped into some form of gravy made of either lentils, peas or cabbage, although sometimes on special occasions chicken or meat. For the local people that was their staple diet, but we were able to vary the diet a little, although when you got meat it had to be cooked in a pressure cooker as I think the animal gave itself up!

Woman baking Injura

The food was heavily spiced and it took quite a while getting used to this, but ultimately we loved this food and years later when we were back in the United Kingdom and especially when we travelled to London, we would go to a restaurant where they sold Ethiopian food.

The local village of Batie consisted mainly of small round houses with a thatched roof. When you arrived at the entrance, there was no door. You were welcomed by a call from inside ግቡ [enter] and when you got inside and got used to the darkness, you discovered a fire burning in the middle of the home with the smoke just trying to get out through the thatched roof. No wonder there were so many people arriving at the clinic with serious eye problems

The house had an inner section where the family ate and slept and an outer section where the sheep and goats and chickens were kept safe from any intruder. There was a large clay pot where the water, which came from the river, was kept and we learned quickly that the only time you took the water from this pot was when it was boiled. As there was no tuberculin testing of the cows, the milk had also to be boiled. It was a completely different way of life.

Woman bringing water from the river

Soon we became accustomed to the sights and smells. Someone had told us to take photos during the first few months in the country as after that you would become so accustomed to the situation - we discovered this to be true. The town of Batie is about 4,000 feet above sea level and sits on the edge of the Great Rift Valley which soon dips down to a desert. When I travelled with John McQuoid to Assab, the sea port, to collect our goods, at one point on the road the altitude seemed to dip very low. When the window of the car was opened it felt like looking into an oven.

It was the Dallol crater, one of the lowest known volcanic vents in the world today, 150 feet (45m) below sea level. The geological depression of the Afar Region continues even lower, eventually reaching 509 feet (155m) below sea level. If you think your job is tough, spare a thought for the men who dig for salt in one of the hottest places on Earth, the so-called 'Gateway to Hell'. Ethiopia is situated in the north east of Africa in what is called the horn of Africa. It is neighbour to South Sudan in the northwest, Eritrea in the north, Somalia in the east and Kenya in the south. Ethiopia was officially called Abyssinia until 1941. The Ethiopia referred to in the Bible was perhaps much larger than it is today and may have included part of Sudan.

Ethiopian history

From 1930 to 1974, Ethiopia was ruled by Emperor Haile Selassie. The most of North Africa is controlled by Islam including Morocco, Algeria, Libya, Egypt, Sudan and Somalia, just to mention a few of these countries. The Ottoman Empire controlled most of north Africa apart from Ethiopia.

It has often been said of Ethiopia that it is **'an island of Christianity in a sea of Islam'**. Today it is surrounded by many difficulties in the neighbouring countries of South Sudan, Eritrea and Somalia.

Judaism was practised in Ethiopia before the Gospel reached that land. The eunuch of Acts chapter 8, who went to Jerusalem to worship the God of the Jews, would probably have been among Ethiopia's earliest Christian believers.

A key person in spreading the Gospel in Ethiopia was a godly Syrian monk called Frumentius, whose work in the 4th century led to Christianity being declared the country's official state religion. The Ethiopian Orthodox Church was the upholder of that religion.

The Ethiopian Orthodox Church is not totally biblical in its beliefs and practices. It is true that the cross is the church's symbol, but salvation is believed to be not simply through faith in Christ, but also by observing numerous Holy Days, by fasting and by praying to God and to the saints, and especially to the intercessory work of Mary, the mother of Jesus.

Muhammad, who founded Islam, was born in Mecca, Arabia, around 570 AD and died in 632 AD. 'Revelations' which he reported as receiving were written down subsequently in the Quran on which the religion of Islam is based and which its followers, Muslims, regard as the 'Word of God'. In Ethiopia today, Islam is growing numerically, in militancy, and in wealth donated by oil-producing countries.

The Ethiopian government did not permit missionaries to work amongst the Ethiopian Orthodox churches and when John Flynn travelled up to Wallo province in the north of the country, having been invited there by the Crown Prince, he felt after much prayer that Batie was the place to commence missionary work.

This included a school which commenced from Grade 1 and ultimately built up to Grade 6 and also to commence a busy clinic. In this new place, they were given permission to preach the Gospel and tried to evangelize among the Muslims. Sadly, very few Muslims trusted in Christ.

Along with Liberia in the west of Africa, Ethiopia was never colonised, although both were taken over for a brief time by a foreign power. Ethiopia was invaded by Italy under Mussolini in 1935. The aim of invading Ethiopia was to boost Italian national prestige, which was wounded by Ethiopia's defeat of Italian forces at the Battle of Adowa in 1896, which saved Ethiopia from Italian colonisation.

It was after Italy joined forces with Germany that Ethiopia was liberated by the British army from Italy in 1941. Emperor Haile Selassie, who had been living in exile in Bath for about 5 years, returned to Ethiopia and ruled there until he was deposed in 1974.

Emperor Haile Selassie's troubles began in 1973 with disquiet in the countryside and in the peasant-based army over Government attempts to hush up a drought that eventually took 100,000 lives in two northern provinces, one of them being Wallo where the Flynns were working.

The unrest was compounded in February 1974, when mutinies broke out in the military over low pay and a secessionist guerrilla war in Eritrea complicated the Emperor's problems. In the spring and summer, after riots in Addis Ababa, his absolute power was taken from him.

A British journalist, Jonathan Dimbleby, visited Ethiopia and took a report of the famine back to Britain. The film which he produced was then used by those opposing Emperor Haile Selassie. The film showing the severe famine was then interspersed by the opposition with large banquets hosted by the Emperor for foreign heads of state in Addis, and it was then shown all over Ethiopia. Emperor Haile Selassie was put under house arrest in September 1974 and died one year later to the day.

The announcement said that his servant had also died on that day so the whole episode was shrouded in mystery and many believed that Emperor Haile Selassie had been suffocated. He was buried in an unmarked grave before the announcement came on the radio. Some years later, his body was exhumed and he was given a state funeral.

As a result of all this change, a communist government came to power and they continued to rule until 1991.

Emperor Haile Selassie – from 1930 - 1974

CHAPTER SIX

Language Learning

Sheena and I were soon immersed in learning the Amharic language, a Semitic language and which is closely related to both Arabic and Hebrew although with different characters. We soon discovered that the original Bible had been translated into Ge'ez, a Semitic language, in the 4th century long before it was translated into English. There are 231 characters in the main alphabet with many other diphthongs as well. Someone has traced the letters in Hebrew to the characters in Amharic, although Amharic is read from left to right.

We were ably taught by John McQuoid and we also had a local tutor who helped us with pronunciation. We soon discovered that there were nuances in the language which were difficult to differentiate, with letters being doubled or rather elongated but not found in the writing.

There were also letters that were exploded, for example k, p, s, t by use of the lips, the tongue or the teeth, the difference being e.g., 'he hit' [explosive] to 'he came' [non explosive]. We learned the basics from John, but it was a long time before we were, as Dan Crawford put it, 'thinking black'.

We also learned that sentences were not written as we knew them in English. **John 3:16 is**

በእርሱ የሚያምን ሁሉ የዘላለም ሕይወት እንዲኖረው እንጂ እንዳይጠፋ እግዚአብሔር አንድያ ልጁን እኪሰጥ ድረስ ዓለምን እንዲሁ ወዶአልና።

The word እግዚአብሔር is the word for God which is half way through the verse, and this word has to be learned very early in conversation as it is used in all forms of greetings. When you are asked how you are, you reply, 'God be praised, I am well'. If someone asks where you are going, you would reply, 'If God wills, I am going to the town'.

The word ወደላትኝ is the word **loved** and you have to wait till the last word before you discover what the main verb is.

Sometime before the language course was completed, John and Valerie McQuoid made it known that they were exercised about commencing a new work serving God in Addis Ababa. Sheena and I with our two children said we would like to join them as we had not completed our language course.

	[ə]	[u]	[i]	[a]	[e]	[ə]	[o]			[ə]	[u]	[i]	[a]	[e]	[ə]	[o]
	ሀ	ሁ	ሂ	ሃ	ሄ	ህ	ሆ			ከ	ኩ	ኪ	ካ	ኬ	ክ	ኮ
	ለ	ሉ	ሊ	ላ	ሌ	ል	ሎ			ወ	ዉ	ዊ	ዋ	ዌ	ው	ዎ
	ሐ	ሑ	ሒ	ሓ	ሔ	ሕ	ሖ			አ	ኡ	ኢ	ኣ	ኤ	እ	ኦ
	መ	ሙ	ሚ	ማ	ሜ	ም	ሞ			ደ	ዱ	ዲ	ዳ	ዴ	ድ	ዶ
	ሠ	ሡ	ሢ	ሣ	ሤ	ሥ	ሦ			ጀ	ጁ	ጂ	ጃ	ጄ	ጅ	ጆ
	ረ	ሩ	ሪ	ራ	ሬ	ር	ሮ			የ	ዩ	ዪ	ያ	ዬ	ይ	ዮ

Part of the Amharic alphabet

There were some amusing incidents during language learning. Sometimes when we were in Addis we would try and spell out what the word was saying in Amharic. One day we saw a rather long word and so we started to spell it out and when we finally deciphered it we discovered it was telecommunication! We also discovered that there were many words in Amharic, and particularly about a motor car, that had Italian background as there were no words in Amharic to cover the parts of a car.

Schooling

When Sheena and I arrived in Batie, it was not long before Crawford began his first year in school at Bingham Academy in September. Bingham Academy was a Christian boarding school run by Sudan Interior Mission [Society of international missionaries].

As it was about 400 kilometres from Batie, it was quite difficult to leave one's child so far from his parents at the age of 7, but Crawford seemed to settle in well at school. We had chatted to Crawford about going off to school and we hoped he was prepared for this new phase of his life.

Jane joined Crawford one year later and Sheena used to say that when she was in Ethiopia, she never saw her children and when they were home on furlough, she never saw her husband! I often wondered what that phrase really meant.

I now believe that was the sacrifice which my beloved wife was prepared to make in the cause of Christ all through our married lives. I thank God for such an understanding wife as we sought to serve God together.

Both Crawford and Jane made many friends at Bingham which they still have maintained over many years, but in thinking back were these friends in the place of Dad and Mum?

I know that when Jane came home to Scotland, she found it difficult to cope, and many days she was so sad that she longed that we would go back to Ethiopia as she had lost her closest friends that had meant so much to her. Coming to a secular Secondary School in Scotland where there were no close friends like at Bingham was a greater cultural shock for Jane than being away in a boarding school in Africa.

Sometimes thoughts pass through your mind many years later that are difficult to come to terms with. Did my dear wife feel let down at times when I wasn't there to support her as I was too busy in the service of God? Thankfully Sheena was always there to see to the needs of the children, for which I am deeply grateful.

How did my children feel being left in a boarding school? There are children now grown up in the United Kingdom who still feel these scars of Dad and Mum not being there when they needed them most.

When we left them at the school gates weeping, did we control our emotions for afterwards, and tell them to do the same, and later on did we pour out our hearts to God and wonder if we had done the right thing? In those days, home schooling didn't seem to have been an option.

After all, we had been called to serve the Lord, but our children hadn't. And are there in the United Kingdom children of missionary parents who have felt let down by missing parental support, feelings that they still harbour in their hearts?

I can think of some missionaries' children who have never come to terms with their past lives, and what is needed most of all is a caring Christian counsellor who can probe into their innermost feelings about the past and be there to give helpful advice.

Are the feelings that I have now, with my beloved taken home to glory and my children a long way away from me, the same feelings that they felt when they were children in being so much alone with no one to share that emptiness?

It is the empty house and the empty chair that I feel most of all. Maybe I have a much more understanding heart now than I had when I was so busy in the service of God, and maybe unconsciously neglected the children.

The fellowship of believers is very meaningful, but it never takes the place of family. Sometimes when I read our past diaries and see how busy I was, I must confess I feel utterly embarrassed and it leaves me thinking……..

Bingham Academy was a wonderful Christian school and it taught the children early in life to have a good interest in the study of the Bible and there was a lovely Christian atmosphere, but it never replaced home.

Samuel Cunningham, Crawford, Gillian Taylor, Flynn boys

It was a great sacrifice not only for the parents but also for the children. Lasting scars could have been left as a result of this sacrifice, but we both thanked God that Crawford and Jane were in some ways able to adjust to life away from Dad and Mum.

When the children had their holidays, they used to come home via Ethiopian Airlines. It was a reasonable price and the airlines used a Twin Otter plane which had about 18 seats. Flying into Combolcha was quite difficult as Combolcha airport was surrounded by mountains. I remember travelling up to Combolcha on a very foggy morning. When we got near our destination, I could see the pilot standing up in the cockpit to look for a gap in the clouds and then dropping down to the airport. The airport was a rough field of grass and sometimes the runway had to be cleared of cattle before the plane could land.

On one occasion I took Jane and some of the other children to Combolcha to meet someone who was coming to visit us. Jane was playing with the other children at the airport terminal which was just a large hut. Unknown to the children, below the hut there was a dog that had rabies and it suddenly came out and bit Jane. Fortunately, it bit her through her clothes, but she had to have many injections in her abdomen to make sure she didn't get rabies. We were relieved parents when she did not succumb to the dreadful disease.

Those first few years in Ethiopia were not easy - adjusting to the climate, learning a new language, leaving your children in a school a long way off. But during this time we also learned about the unfailing faithfulness of God in all that we were seeking to do.

One of the many examples of His faithfulness was when we were in Addis while the McQuoids were on furlough. At this particular time, we were due to pay the fees for the children's education at Bingham Academy, but we didn't have the money to pay for the fees.

We committed this matter to the Lord in prayer that morning. About 9am we had a telephone call from a Mr Robinson who told us that he worked with the children's fund of the UN and he was on business in Addis. He wondered if he could come and see us in the evening. I said that we would be delighted to see him and I would pick him up at his hotel and he could spend a few hours at our home.

I picked up brother Robinson and we discovered that he was one of the trustees in USA of Christian Missions in Many Lands and he was keen to learn how we were doing in Addis.

It transpired that he had come with his wife to London and while there he had telephoned Echoes of Service to ask if there were any missionaries in Addis. He was told that the Revies were there and he was given our telephone number. He could quite easily have been given our post box number and we might never have met.

We spent a lovely evening with this brother whom we had never met nor have we seen him since, although we later learned that his daughter went to South Africa as a missionary.

I then took brother Robinson back to his hotel and, as we were parting, he slipped something into my top shirt pocket. It was not until I got home that I discovered that it was a cheque and the amount was the exact figure for the children's fees at Bingham. It was then we learned practically the truth of the verse of Scripture, **'Before they call, I will answer, and while they are yet speaking, I will hear' (Isa. 65:4).**

We discovered in our own experience that our greatest difficulties were in our first year in Ethiopia. We were new missionaries and were unknown apart from the places in Ayrshire and West Lothian where we had spent most of our time before going abroad.

But we felt that the Lord was just testing us to get us to rely wholly on Him for our support, and during all our missionary service the Lord has never failed us, and for this we are so grateful.

We both felt that having the responsibility in Addis of seeking to maintain a new service for God and seeking to develop it, we were grateful that God used us in this way, although at times we felt we had been thrown in at the deep end.

During this time, I was the representative for the missionaries with regard to work permits etc. and that took some time as well.

CHAPTER SEVEN

Moving to Dagan

After the language course had been completed in April 1970, we moved to Dagan to help Ron and Maria Cunningham who had just commenced a work there and we were invited to join them in this new venture, especially for work in the clinic. I went along to see the piece of ground that had been rented to Ron to have the clinic and the school.

The village of Dagan is about 20 kilometres from Batie and at that time there was no medical work there at all. There was nothing in the large field that was given to the Cunninghams for the clinic and the school so a house had to be built for Ron and Maria.

There was no electricity in this field where we were and so again we were reduced to an oil lamp for our lighting. However, when John Harkness, a dear brother from Northern Ireland, heard about the situation while we were on furlough, he very kindly sent a generator for the work of God at Dagan. When the generator arrived, the locals got some logs and it was rolled down the hill until it reached the small shed where it was bolted to the floor.

I had been given instructions from Jim McCurdie some time before on how to produce a 13 amp ring circuit, so I went about wiring all the houses. The generator was then switched on and amazingly everything worked! This was left for the local people when all the missionaries left Dagan in 1978.

We went along to Dagan from Batie to help Ron finish his house. I went along with John Flynn to help to put the roof on.

Tragedy at Dagan

It was 9th April 1970 and the medical work hadn't really commenced. The day was dull with the possibility of rain. Dagan lies in a valley and is surrounded by mountains. When the rain came it could be seen for a few hours prior to it sweeping down the valley towards Dagan. The house was almost complete - all that was needed was a few corrugated sheets to be added to the roof. Just as the roof was being completed, a hurricane hit the house with such force that the whole house was raised to the ground. I was on the roof one moment helping to nail down the final sheets, and the next moment I was on the ground.

John Flynn and Ron Cunningham too were very shocked and we hardly knew what had happened. Shortly afterwards, once I gained my breath I heard someone calling 'Daddy' and I knew that at least one person was buried under the house.

I had no tools as they were now buried under the rubble, so I made my way between the roof and the ceiling until I identified where the calls were coming from. Finally, I was able to break the bamboo with my hands and found Samuel Cunningham safe and well but sadly, near to him, lay two Ethiopian boys who had been killed when the house collapsed.

I sustained a serious injury on my right hand as the bamboo had cut right into one of my fingers. I suffered agony for a day, then it was decided that I should fly to Addis to get additional medical help. When I got to the Hospital, they decided to operate as I had severe cellulitis. After the operation, because of the way the dressings were put on, I was left with the injured finger in a very cramped position which made it almost impossible to grip items like a hammer.

Some time later, I had a friend who worked in the large leprosarium in Addis and he told me that a Swiss surgeon, a Dr Fritchie, working in India with Dr Paul Brand, was coming to Addis and he was willing to see me. Dr Fritchie said he could operate and he did an excellent job on my right finger. The problem can only now be seen when the hand is in the rigid position.

This injury left me with a scar on my right hand, and often when speaking to children I would tell them that I had a scar on one of my hands in an attempt to save one person, whereas the Lord Jesus had scars on both His hands in order to provide salvation for the world.

This was a serious blow at the beginning of this new work of serving God, but the local people took it well and said they felt that this was an act of God. Gladly, it did not affect the work of both the clinic and the school.

It wasn't long till we decided to build a house for ourselves. I along with local labourers began to build our house which cost us around £500. During the construction of the house, we lived in a caravan given to us by Willie and Nan Milliken and I built a lean-to which Sheena used as a kitchen.

Often we would hear and see large rats scrambling across the wood on the roof in search of any food that may have been left out. Sadly, one night a hurricane hit the caravan and the lean-to was swept away and we had to quickly rush for shelter in the Cunningham's house.

The first task in building a house was to form a frame using undressed wood as the basic structure. This was then filled in with bamboo, leaving a space of a finger width between each piece of bamboo. A large pit was dug which was then filled with straw and mud and water which was then allowed to ferment.

The local men said that 'if it didn't smell, it didn't stick'. During this process the mud etc. was mixed by the workers by going into the pit and tramping the contents with their bare feet. When ready, the mud was made into balls and thrown at the outer side of the wall and then left to dry. Then mud was applied on the inner side of the wall and it produced an effect that was similar to the lath and plaster used in the United Kingdom before the 1940s. After all this was completed, a final coat of mud was applied which made the walls reasonably smooth.

Finally, a corrugated roof was added to complete the house with a ceiling being made of bamboo and mud as well. The house was then painted with whitewash and as the mud proved good insulation the house was cool in the hot season and warm when the cool season came, so it was an ideal material for use in Ethiopia

After we spent one year with Ron and Maria, we returned to Addis to oversee the work that John and Valerie had recently commenced as they left for furlough in June 1971. A small assembly had been formed and we were left in charge of this work in the capital. I started Bible studies with nurses in two of the hospitals in Addis. These were both very well attended and it was felt that a number of lives were changed as a result of these studies.

Our house at Dagan - £500

At that time Willie and Nan Milliken, who had been involved in running a medical clinic down in a cotton plantation at a place called Dubtie about 100 km south of Batie, had moved to Addis and they were in charge of a hostel in the capital.

These were encouraging times when many doors were opened for preaching and teaching and a Gospel meeting was commenced on a Sunday evening. Sheena and I became very friendly with a number of brethren in the capital who were able preachers of the Gospel.

Sadly, Valerie McQuoid, after the birth of their third child Jeremy, was quite unwell and as a result the McQuoids delayed their return to Ethiopia for one more year and they returned in 1973.

Sheena and I decided that we would go for a furlough in May 1973. We were at home for one year and lived with Sheena's parents in Tarbolton and so it was nice for them to get to know their grandchildren. It was then that we really appreciated the sacrifice that is made not only by the missionaries but by their parents in not seeing their children and grandchildren for a number of years.

At this time, Sheena was pregnant with our third child and it was a mercy that we had travelled home as she had severe pre-eclampsia fairly soon after we arrived in Scotland. We had been in London for a few days holiday with the children when Sheena felt very unwell. We then decided to return immediately to Scotland and we went to stay with my brother Willie and his wife Annie in Perth.

Willie often visited auction sales and he had just acquired a blood pressure machine and a stethoscope, so when we arrived at his home I took Sheena's blood pressure and discovered it was very high. We immediately telephoned the local doctor and when he saw Sheena, he sent her right away into Perth hospital where she was for the next six weeks.

Sheena was not well during her stay in hospital and I was glad when the consultant decided to do a Caesarean section. It was then that Norman our third child was born prematurely in September 1973 weighing about 2 kg.

When Jane saw him in his incubator, she said he was like 'a skinned rabbit' and so he was, but he soon made good progress and subsequently never showed that he had been a premature baby. Norman stayed in the hospital after Sheena was allowed home and it was a great day when we were able to take him back to Tarbolton.

Return to Ethiopia

After a year in the Unitrd Kingdom, it was time to return to Ethiopia. One of the first things we had to do in Addis before going up country was to buy some linoleum for the floor as we could not have a baby crawling on the concrete floor.

When we returned from the UK we had with us Ann Reed. Ann had a desire to be of some help to the work of God on the mission field, and when she heard about our work she offered to come for six months.

When we went to Dagan and opened the door of our house, I will never forget Ann's eyes as she viewed the scene. The malaria eradication team had visited our house while we were on furlough and there was a fine white dust over all the furniture. It took the three of us some time to get things back to normal.

After Ann had completed her general nurses training, she completed a course in ophthalmics in Moorfield's Eye Hospital in London. Her experience in this field was so beneficial in Ethiopia as we had many patients with eye problems. Ann was able to see these patients and sometimes if necessary she would perform minor surgery on their eyes. When Ann returned to the United Kingdom she met an American airman, Lance Lordanich. After some time she contacted me and asked if I would marry them.

I was happy to do this and we had a lovely wedding in Oxford. They are very happy in San Diego and Sheena and I visited Lance and Ann when we were in the States and spent a very nice time with them.

At the same time, we also had staying with us Elizabeth Brown whose parents Michael and Grace Brown had spent many years in the Far East in missionary work. Elizabeth fitted in so well to the work in Ethiopia and she was able to do many tasks that freed the rest of us to spend more time in other ways.

When we returned to Ethiopia in May 1974, there was much unrest in the country. A famine was at its height in Wallo province in the north east of Ethiopia. Bill and Kath Taylor were doing sterling work seeking to help those who were suffering from malnutrition in a camp at a place called Combolcha about 20 km from Dagan.

It was so sad to see so many people absolutely destitute and desperately needing both medical and practical help. The Taylors were able to pour into these dear souls the 'balm of Gilead' and to show love and kindness. We feel that many people were touched by this show of Christian love.

CHAPTER EIGHT
Medical Work

As Ron and Maria and Sheena and I were nurses and the ladies were midwives it was decided that the couples would take alternate weeks in the clinic. When not in the clinic, visits were made into the countryside where often there was arranged an informal gathering in a village where people gathered to hear the Word of God. Sadly, during this time, there was quite a bit of opposition from the local witch doctor in the village of Dagan.

However, a serious bout of cholera affected the area and when the people who had contracted cholera went to the witch doctor he told them that he could not help them and they should go to the foreigners. At that time many very seriously ill patients came to the clinic and a tent had to be erected for them and amazingly not one patient died. Thus the reputation of the clinic became recognised over a wide area.

The clinic also provided vaccination against cholera and every morning around 1,000 people gathered to receive the vaccinations. The Ethiopians felt that if you got one injection, two would be better, and so they went in one door and then left only to come back in for a second jag. When it was discovered what was happening the nursing staff put some gentian violet on the injection site so that when they came in for a second time they were told that one was enough!

About 600 patients were seen every week. They had to be registered, examined and diagnosed then prescriptions were given. Various diseases were common among those who came such as tuberculosis, leprosy, venereal diseases, and ring and tape worm. Most of the maternity patients that Sheena and Maria saw were those who had been unable to give birth at home and they faced many difficult and very serious situations.

There were also many local practices that Maria and Sheena soon became aware of. One day after Sheena had delivered a baby, she came into the room where the baby was and discovered that there was blood on the baby's ear. What the mother had done was to cut a bit off the baby's ear to help her become pregnant again. The mother was given a severe reprimand and an explanation that what she had done had no medical backing.

On another occasion, a woman came into the clinic and said that the afterbirth was still in the womb. When Sheena examined the lady, she could hear a heart-beat and she told the lady that there was still another baby in the womb. Shortly after this, the lady gave birth to another baby and they were delighted at the outcome. As this was about three days after the initial birth, some doctors who visited us said that this was medical history and we should have written something about it.

I had met a very helpful dentist in the United Kingdom who showed me how to treat dental problems. Also a dentist in Aberdeen sent a dentist's chair to Ethiopia and as a result many patients were treated with tooth problems. The main problem was that some local witch doctor had tried to take out the offending tooth and in the process had broken the head of the tooth. I had the job of extracting the roots - sometimes it took a while but I always seemed to manage.

We often saw patients who had serious medical conditions which were away beyond our ability to treat, but the Lord seemed to give us that extra help in such difficult cases. Often the relatives would say that if we didn't help them, they would take the patient home to die as they had no confidence in the local hospital.

One man who had been working at a cotton plantation in Dubtie, about two hours from Dagan, was bitten five times by a venomous snake. He had been picking cotton and suddenly he saw the snake and he tried to hit it with his stick. Unfortunately he missed it and when he arrived at the clinic, he was swollen all over like 'The Michelin Man'.

However, we took him into our home and treated each crisis as it presented itself, and it was a great day when the man walked out of the clinic completely healed. He became a lorry driver and each time he passed he would stop and present us with a gift in appreciation of the help he had been given.

On another occasion, a man arrived at the clinic and he looked physically drained. He had been gored by an ox and the wound had punctured his abdomen. We did our best by binding him up with warm clean bindings and then took him to the local hospital 60 km away although we felt that he would never survive. Sometime later, Valerie McQuoid came to our home and with her was a man who was carrying some bananas to give us as a gift and it turned out that this was our man who had been gored by the ox.

One Saturday after the market in Dagan, after drinking too much of the local alcohol, a man was brought to the clinic with a wound in his back from a large knife which just missed the spinal cord by about an inch. His lung was also punctured. I stitched him up and wondered if he would ever survive.

Many years later, when we returned to Ethiopia in 1993 we were in a taxi going to Batie when a man asked me if I was the tall nurse who used to work in the Dagan clinic. When I said I was, the man pulled off his shirt and showed me the wound that I had stitched up years before. He was most grateful for what I had done.

There were other sad situations when a woman may have become pregnant by another man, not her husband, and in order to have an abortion she would take local medicine. But often she took too much which resulted in her death. During Ramadan, the month when Muslims do not eat anything between sunrise and sunset, and many would not even swallow their saliva, you had to be aware of them spitting in the clinic. Added to that many would not even be willing to take medicine during the day so you had to tell them how to take the medicine during the night. No matter how many tablets of antibiotics you gave to the patients, unless they also were given an injection, they thought the tablets would not work. So we would give them an injection of a vitamin and they went away happy and took the tablets.

Crawford's Secondary Schooling

In 1976, a new situation had to be addressed. Crawford had now reached the point in his schooling when Sheena and I had to decide which route to take to further his education. After some discussion and much prayer, it was decided that Crawford would go back to Scotland and stay with his Uncle Willie and Aunt Annie who lived in Perth, and continue his secondary education there.

Unfortunately, the curriculum at Bingham Academy was different from Scotland particularly in mathematics when only one of the maths subjects was studied per year at Bingham. This meant that Crawford was missing one of his maths subjects. However, when Crawford and I arrived in Perth it was discovered he had hepatitis. This meant that he had to remain at home for six weeks.

Crawford's cousin Craig was scheduled to go to university in October of that year and so he tutored Crawford through the missing maths subject in six weeks bringing Crawford up to date with his maths! He spent two years with his uncle and aunt and during this time he made an acquaintance with a young lady called Fiona Christie whom he subsequently married.

We were so appreciative of what my brother Willie and his wife Annie did for Crawford during these two years living in their home. After the two years were completed, we returned home from Ethiopia and Crawford joined us in the Annbank missionary home in Ayrshire.

It was lovely to be back home, to spend some quality time with our family members, and to be able to visit the many assemblies that had supported us during our first term on the mission field. At that time there was a very good missionary interest, but one feels that this interest has waned a bit and there doesn't seem to be the interest that there once was.

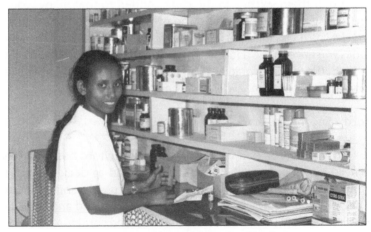

Alimaz one of our helpers in the clinic

Bringing a patient from 6 hours away

CHAPTER NINE

Communist Rule

It was during 1973-91 that a new communist government controlled Ethiopia. They sent out students into the countryside to cause as much chaos as they could. The missionaries had had a good relationship with the local people, but one day Ron and I were called to the local council offices where we were accused of being CIA agents because we were in touch with America.

They said that we had in one of our homes a device that could communicate with America. When we asked to see where this device was, we were taken to Ron's house and the offending item was identified. When John Flynn had left Ethiopia earlier that year, he had left in Ron's care a loudspeaker and this was the device they were alluding to. When we explained that this was a simple loudspeaker, we were allowed to go free!

It was very difficult working during these five years under the new communist government, and the first pressure that was brought to bear on the work at Dagan was that the authorities insisted on teaching communism in the school.

They were told that as this was a Christian school it was impossible to teach communism, so they stated that the teachers' work permits would not be renewed. Some months afterwards, the authorities returned to look at the medical work and see what was done there.

They said they were not interested in the leprosy work, nor did they feel the need for the TB unit, and the work among the maternity patients was unnecessary. They stated that they would not give any replacement visas for nurses who might want to relieve those working in the clinic.

Reluctantly, as all the missionaries became aware that the government no longer wanted us in Ethiopia, we decided to leave the country in May of 1978. It was a sad day when the Cunninghams, Mary Breeze and ourselves left Ethiopia. On that morning, a very large crowd of people gathered and it was so touching to see big bandits with their guns and bullets round their waist, weeping and pleading with us missionaries to remain.

Sadly, the time had come for all to leave. On that morning, most of us felt that the way communism had taken such a hold in the country we would never be back. We were to learn subsequently that **'He which had begun a good work in them would perform it until the day of Jesus Christ'.**

Difficult days

It was so sad to leave a small struggling assembly in Dagan with about 15-20 believers. The same could have been said for the other two assemblies in Batie and Addis Ababa where the total number of believers at that time in the three assemblies was around 100.

Shortly after the missionaries left, the three halls were taken over by the government. One was used as a mill and another was used as a public house and the hall in Dagan was never returned and the believers then went underground.

During this time, it was very difficult for the believers. Many were imprisoned and some were beaten, and others were killed while in prison. One brother called Tesfae from Addis, who had become a head teacher in a school and who was an excellent preacher helping with the work in Addis, was taken and beaten and sadly as a result of this he died.

The believers could only meet with up to five people, as more than that was 'an unlawful assembly'. Added to that, the authorities kept a close watch on all that was going on. The believers during this time could not sing, could only pray very quietly and they never showed openly that they were carrying a Bible.

They always arrived at a safe house individually, and they were always suspicious of anyone who wanted to join the group as he might have come from the security service. If the group reached more than five they started a new group, and there were always severe penalties for those who housed these groups.

A great change came in 1991. The believers were now so happy to be able to sing out loud, to be able to attend services without any fear, to be able to carry their Bibles openly. From that year until now there has been complete freedom to engage in a spiritual ministry.

Sadly, this has not been the case in the country of Eritrea which was once part of Ethiopia. There has been severe persecution against Christians, with many being put in prison in very trying circumstances.

Those who were able tried to leave the country and desired to travel to Europe. Sadly, many never made it. Some lost their lives as they took the long journey through the hostile countries of Sudan and Egypt.

When we arrived back in Addis Ababa in 1993 the hall in Gofa Sifir had been handed back to the believers. Before then it had been very difficult to get much information from the believers as all letters were censored. But a sudden change of events took place in 1991 - that must wait till another chapter.

Eritreans trying to escape from persecution

During the communist control many Jews called **Falasha Jews** were allowed to travel to Israel.

Falasha Jews arriving in Israel

CHAPTER TEN
Change of Service

When Sheena and I returned home to Scotland, we set up home in Tarbolton so that we might be a help to Sheena's parents as at that time her Mum was not too well. It was during the next few months that I was deeply exercised as to what the Lord wanted me to do in further service for the Lord.

When I was a teenager, I was involved in a tract band which numbered into the 30s and on a Saturday afternoon we would visit villages in Ayrshire by bicycle for leaflet distribution and open air preaching. There was a spirit of enthusiasm and a desire to reach villages where there was no assembly and at that time much seed was sown in these villages.

While I was at Ballochmyle, I spent some time helping Willie Scott of Machermore Eventide Home at Newton Stewart. Willie Scott had commenced this Eventide Home in 1953, but he was also involved in evangelising the small villages in the south of Scotland. This gave me the burden of being involved in evangelism with both children and adults.

I remembered that on my first visit to Newton Stewart after a very bumpy ride by bus when I felt very sick, I was met by Willie Scott who at a very fast pace [Willie was a fast driver] took me to the home to meet a number of other brethren who had come to help in evangelism. Among them were David Smith, Boyd Aitken, David and Robert Muir, the Stirrat brothers, Jim Legge, and Alan and John Jack.

On the first evening, Willie Scott took us to a village called Glentrool. We were not long commenced when he passed the microphone to me to give a message. I was a bit embarrassed as I hadn't done too much preaching in the open air in Prestwick.

I wasn't long speaking when I could see all the other young men leaving the ring and going into Willie's car. I thought that this was most disrespectful of them - until finally I discovered I could not continue to preach as a swarm of midges had descended on the village. When I entered the car, Willie was smiling and he said 'Lesson number 1, when you're preaching in the open air, be brief!'

As a result of this introduction to evangelism, when I was about 19, along with two other brethren from the Glenburn assembly, I became involved in organising a holiday for young men when they could continue a similar mode of evangelism. As a result a tent was bought from John James of Tipton along with many seats, platform etc.

The first place that we chose was Eastriggs in the south of Scotland near Annan where there was a small assembly. A local farmer gave us permission to erect the tent in one of his fields and many young men were introduced to this type of evangelism. The farmer's wife did a lot of home baking and sent us scones, pancakes etc. - they were most kind to us.

The mornings were spent organising children's services on the village green, and the brethren hired the local village hall where evening Gospel services were held. On a number of occasions, it was filled with local people. A real work of God was done in that village when some of the teenagers trusted in Christ and I felt that if someone had gone to that area to live it could have been developed even further.

A number of brethren ultimately went out in the Lord's work both at home and abroad. I can remember having fellowship both at Machermore and Eastriggs with Willie Milliken, David Smith, Boyd Aitken, Jim Legge, Robert Muir, Jack Ritchie, David Locke and John Speirs, all of whom later on went into the work of the Lord. It was felt that many lives were touched at an early age as a result of these ministries.

As I had been involved in a pioneer ministry, both in the South of Scotland as a younger man, and also in Ethiopia, I was exercised to continue in this way and as a result I became involved in pioneer evangelism in Ayrshire. At first I began to use local public halls, but because these halls were only available at certain times in the week, I felt that another method was necessary.

As a result, I had a sectional portable hall built by David Watson who had a builder's business at Crosshouse, where Robert Gibson provided much of the skill for completing this first sectional portable hall. It was erected for the first time in Kilmaurs and at the commencement of the work of God it was rather discouraging.

At the beginning, on some of the nights nobody came to the hall neither believer nor unbeliever and I must say I felt a little despondent. It was a real test of my commitment to this kind of work.

However, things improved during the next few weeks and some nights the hall was filled to capacity when Ian Wallace and Rutherford Rabey brought some unsaved young people from Kilbirnie to the portable hall.

During my time in Kilmaurs, I met a lady called Mary Ritchie who told me she was afraid of meeting people in public. She told me that she had been reading her Bible and was at that time reading in the book of the Acts. When she spoke about some of the things she had been reading, it was obvious that this was no cursory reading of Scripture.

In time, she received courage to attend the portable hall and on her first night at the hall she trusted the Saviour. I began to have a weekly Bible study in her home and before I commenced the Bible study one morning Jack, Mary's husband, said he wanted to trust the Saviour. Both were baptised in the Crosshouse Gospel hall and continued there till both were called home. I was also put in touch with the rest of the family and this had an effect on some of the other members.

The portable hall at that time when not in use was stored in the hayshed of Maurice Harrison, a local farmer who was in the assembly in Tarbolton. One day when Maurice was welding outside the hayshed, a spark jumped inside and set the hay on fire. The fire raged all night and the portable hall was completely destroyed after only one year in use.

That was a sad day for the Harrison family as they had a great burden to reach unevangelised villages. This was evident in the years that followed when they supported the portable hall wherever it was pitched.

First portable hall

New portable hall

The same night that the hall was destroyed, I attended a meeting in Kilmarnock and a brother gave me a gift toward the purchase of a new portable hall. When the new hall was completed, all the money had been gifted for its completion.

It was thought that a change in design might be better for the hall, and ultimately it was decided to build a hall made of aluminium. This was in two sections built on a chassis of four wheels. In the building of this hall, I received great help from an Aluminium company called John Adams & Co. in Glasgow who were believers.

Second portable hall

After about 9 months, the new portable hall was finished and ready for service. For the next 23 years the new sectional building was towed to and from each site by Maurice Harrison from Tarbolton and Cecil Foster from Galston, which was a tremendous help to the work of evangelism in Ayrshire.

Sometimes, modifications were needed - one such was that the roof had been built with a very slight incline. However Jim Milne, a dear brother from Aberdeen, took the portable hall to his factory and put on a new fibreglass sloping roof. Sometimes children would pierce the tyres so aprons had to be fitted round the hall to protect the tyres. Another problem was graffiti and this had to be painted out at fairly frequent intervals.

The hall was used mainly in Ayrshire. It was taken to a village for a month where there was either no assembly or a very small one. I had some exceptionally encouraging campaigns in Patna, Girvan, Mauchline and Logan just to mention a few, when unbelievers came under the sound of the Gospel and a number were converted.

After being in Mauchline for four weeks and some had been saved, it was felt that a weekly Bible study should be commenced. Archie & Wilma Hill opened their home for this purpose and as a result of these meetings the Hills with their children came into the assembly at Tarbolton for some years.

When I had meetings in Patna with John Speirs, on a number of nights a good many teenagers attended the meetings. One night a young man came along wearing a leather jacket with several badges of different pop groups. One night I noticed one which looked almost identical to the badges we gave to the children with a text written on it. I thought that this young man had taken a badge from one of the children but on closer inspection I read the words on the badge. It said 'Jesus died for His own sins not mine'.

I said to the young man that this was blasphemy and I would be afraid to wear such a badge. He took it off and didn't wear it again. I was so grieved to think that a factory somewhere in the United Kingdom was producing these badges for sale. However his mother discovered that he had been attending the portable hall and she noticed he had been given some literature.

When he had gone up to bed one night, she began to read the booklets. At about 3am she fell down on the floor and cried to God to take away her sins and she was gloriously converted. For some time she attended the Gospel Hall in Patna, then she became associated with a Pentecostal group and for some time she was involved in taking food and aid to Romania.

After the meetings in Patna, when a number had been converted, I conducted a Bible study on a Friday night for over two years. This also happened in Stewarton when we had a good group coming along to a weekly Bible study.

The hall was taken to Inverkip for four weeks on one occasion, and that began a work in that village that had lasting consequences when a number trusted the Saviour. Miss Grace Stenhouse was deputy head in the local primary school and was a great help to the work. When the meetings in the portable hall were finished, I was able to continue holding children's meetings in Inverkip for a week once a year in the primary school with very good attendances and at least one child was converted at these meetings.

The method that was adopted in the portable hall was to hold adult meetings from Sunday to Thursday and also to hold meetings for children from Monday to Thursday. At the commencement of this ministry I was on my own and it was not easy.

From time to time I was helped by various brethren, including Malcolm Radcliffe, Colin Raggett and Colin's brother David, Sandy Brownlee, and later on in 1989 I was joined by Ian Robertson from Auchinleck for a number of very fruitful years. We visited a number of villages in Ayrshire, including Kilmaurs, Mauchline, Maybole, Muirkirk just to mention a few, where we saw the Lord working in blessing and salvation.

The work among children proved particularly encouraging. On many occasions and in many places the portable hall was filled to capacity, and in spite of the fact that many of these children had never been to a Sunday School the behaviour was very reasonable on most occasions.

In later years when I was conducting Gospel meetings in Crosshill, I visited one afternoon the next village of Dailly. It was a rather wet afternoon and there hadn't been too much interest that day on the doors. However, as I knocked the last door a lady came to the door, and I invited her to the meetings in Crosshill. She said she was sure she knew me, but I felt she was mistaken. Finally, she said to me 'The Portacabin'. Then she went on to tell me that when I had meetings in Dailly in the portable hall about 20 years earlier she had attended the children's meetings and as a result of perfect attendance and saying her memory verses she was given a Bible.

Although it had been so many years before, she remembered that one night I had held up my black Bible and asked the children if they had a READ Bible. As a girl she remembered that when the children said it was a black Bible I had explained that there were two ways to spell read. It could be RED the colour, or READ being the past tense of read. The lady confessed that the Bible she had been given wasn't a read Bible all that often, but I was so encouraged to think she had remembered this after so many years.

After some time Ian Robertson felt that the Lord was calling him and Mary to set up a new work for drug addicts and alcoholics in Auchinleck and they continued in this work for several years afterwards.

After 23 years working in the portable hall, sometimes having to do the work on my own, I felt that the time had come to draw this service to a close. This decision was also influenced by the fact that I was becoming more involved with the work in Ethiopia, for apart from the regular three monthly visits I made there was also a need for editing the many books that were being translated into Amharic.

I was very glad when some believers from Northern Ireland said they could use the hall for work among children, so it was transported there and has continued to be of service in another part of the United Kingdom.

During all these years in the portable hall and engaging in Gospel campaigns in other parts of the United Kingdom, I was away from home many times and Sheena supported me in all the work I was engaged in. Only once did Sheena complain about me being away from home.

It was the year 1986 and I was in Stoke on Trent having a campaign in a tent during the month of May and I stayed in a caravan beside the tent. It just happened that this was our 25th wedding anniversary and Sheena said she would never let me forget this. I felt quite ashamed that I had overlooked this special date in my diary.

When it came to our 40th anniversary, Sheena asked to see my diary and she put a big cross through the month of September. We then spent a wonderful month together visiting Canada and the USA, incorporating visits to some friends that we had known while in Ethiopia.

From 1979 to 2007, I was involved in camp work in different parts of Scotland, England and Wales. I spent a number of years with the Aberdeen Camp and also the North Staffs Camp, being at both of them more than seven years. In later years, I met many young folk who had either been saved at camp or their lives had been challenged at camp and this guided them to become more involved in the service of God. These times in so many different camps in the United Kingdom greatly helped me when camps were set up in Ethiopia.

CHAPTER ELEVEN

Amazing Changes

It was in 1991 that the world looked on in amazement at the fall of communism in Russia. Little did anyone realise that this would have important repercussions in other parts of the world including Ethiopia which was so dependent on Russia. In 1991 the communist government in Ethiopia was overthrown and a new government came into power.

This enabled Sheena and me to return to Ethiopia in 1993 for three months with a tourist visa, and we did this for the next 20 years or so. When we returned to Ethiopia, we found that the small assembly in Gofa Sifir of 30 had now increased to over 300. We were truly delighted to see this progress.

In 1991 when the communist government was overthrown, the brethren who met in Addis were keen to develop a work for God in the area west of Addis at a place called Ginchi, about 90 km from Addis. By 2015, there were assemblies formed in all the towns along the road from Ginchi to Addis Ababa and a special conference was held then to thank God for the development of the work in that area.

In 1992, Crawford, our oldest child, was in Ethiopia on work relating to his lecturing post at Glasgow University. One day he went into a Post Office at a place called Arat Kilo which is quite a bit away from the centre of Addis. He asked the assistant, in Amharic, for a number of stamps.

The man asked him how long he had been in Ethiopia, and when Crawford said he had been there three days, the man then asked him how he could speak Amharic. Crawford told the assistant that his parents had been missionaries in Ethiopia. When the assistant asked where they had been working, he told him it was at Dagan about 400 km from Addis. From behind the counter a voice cried, 'Are you Mr Revie's son?' This was Mohammed Said.

Mohammed was a boy from Dagan and his father was one of the Muslim Sheiks in Dagan. He and Crawford had often played together. Mohammed joined the school managed by Mary Breeze. He was a particularly bright boy with a very good memory. He also came to the Sunday School and was able to memorise all the Bible verses. He then moved to the High School in the next town, Combolcha. He did so well that he was given a place in the university at that time in Addis Ababa.

Mohammed was keen to become a doctor, but it was at the time when the communist government decided which course you took and he was given the subject of social sciences. He was not all that keen on this subject and one of his teachers noticed this. In his second year he was given poor marks in his exams and was told to leave the university. By this time he had rejected Islam and also what he learned in Sunday School, and had become a communist cadre.

Mohammed discovered that he could continue his education in a university in Bulgaria so off he went there. But after some time he discovered it was only to get cheap labour and as a result he left Bulgaria and returned to Ethiopia and got this job in the Post Office in Arat Kilo. What a coincidence for Mohammed to meet Crawford in a big city like Addis! Crawford told Mohammed that his parents were coming to Ethiopia in January 1993, and Mohammed asked Crawford to tell his parents to call to see him.

When we arrived in Ethiopia, one of the first places we visited was the Post Office to find Mohammed. By this time he had rejected communism and he told me that he had begun to study the Bible again. That first visit was the beginning of many discussions over many weeks for long hours, and this resulted in Mohammed trusting the Saviour at the end of the three months.

We got an email from Mohammed 9 months later to tell us that he was getting married to a girl called Membere who was the secretary in the office of the assemblies. Mohammed felt that we were now his spiritual parents and he wanted us to be at his wedding and he gave us the date. We then replied that we hoped he would have a lovely wedding, but we had to delay our return to Ethiopia and as a result would not be able to attend his wedding. Mohammed then sent another email to say that they would just change the date of the wedding so that we could attend!

Just around this time, Sheena was contacted by a sister who was about to close her shop. She had sold wedding dresses and she wondered if Sheena had any use for the ones that were left. The previous year some sisters in Ethiopia had mentioned to Sheena that a number of believers who were poor did not have the money to pay for a wedding dress, and they often had to hire one which was quite expensive. As a result Sheena took a number of these dresses, including one for Membere, to Ethiopia. I had also managed to get a suit for Mohammed.

At that time we were travelling to Ethiopia by Lufthansa Airways, but the flight from the United Kingdom had been delayed by 45 minutes. I told one of the stewards that we were travelling on to Ethiopia and hoped to catch another flight in Frankfurt. The steward said he would contact the airline to make sure we got our flight. When I asked about our luggage he told me that they couldn't be sure of getting it onto the plane bound for Addis on that day. He also said that there was a flight going out on Saturday and our luggage may be delayed and would arrive then.

Mohammed and family

However, I told the steward that we were going to a wedding on the Saturday and we had the bride's dress in our luggage. When we arrived in Addis, we were delighted to see our luggage. We attended the wedding and had a wonderful time. Mohammed and Membere are now living in Saris just south of the capital and they are a great help in that assembly.

In 1993, the believers were able to meet once more in public and sing openly and they were able to carry their Bibles in public. At this time the assembly in Gofa Sifir was meeting in the original hall which had just been returned to them, but it was in need of much repair. It was also too small for the congregation so two services were held on the Sunday morning. I remember the first conference I attended when the hall was packed. There was a very poor loud-speaking equipment which crackled a lot, and when I suggested it be turned off I was told that there were more people outside the hall than there were inside!

The believers were able to pull down the old hall and build a new one. Before they could do that, some people who had taken up residence in our property had to be evicted and find other accommodation. This involved the exchange of some money. The Gofa Sifir believers were given a substantial gift towards this building through the help of brother John McQuoid who had commenced the work at Gofa Sifir about 20 years earlier.

At this time the person who was co-ordinating my visit was Solomon Abebe who had spent some time in the assembly at Batie. After one year Solomon moved on to work for a Christian organisation called Great Commision [Campus crusade] promoting the use of Bible films and his place was taken by Mulugeta Ashagre.

During this first visit, we gradually became aware of the changed situation in the country. There was now an assembly at Gofa Sifir, at Saris, one in Wilincomi, and a small hall had just been bought in Ginchi where a small group was meeting, and there was also a group of believers meeting in Akaki. The hall in Batie had not been returned to the believers and the hall in Dagan was never returned. Some of the believers in Dagan had died, some had moved to other areas and sadly some had reverted to Islam. In these early days, there were seven assemblies in the country.

During this our first trip we stayed with **Mary Breeze**. Mary was a school teacher who had worked with us at Dagan. When all the missionaries left the country, Mary had joined Wycliffe translators and after some time had been posted back to Ethiopia. She was living in rented premises in Addis which had two bedrooms, and on all our trips for the next 20 years she gave us the use of one of these bedrooms. This was ideal because when I went out to the countryside Sheena was able to stay with Mary. Mary was willing to share her home in Addis during all this time until she retired from Wycliffe and returned to England when other arrangements had to be made. We were indebted to Mary who did such a service for us over all these years.

When we returned to Ethiopia in the second year, things had changed. A new co-ordinator had been appointed and for the next 20 years or so my itinerary was arranged by Mulugeta Ashagre with whom we have worked in real unity like a father and a son.

Mulugeta lived in the province of Kaffa. His father had a reasonable sized farm but when the communist government came to power he lost all his land. About this time, Mulugeta was sent to Addis to continue his education and he stayed with one of his uncles.

Mulugeta and Alumnish

Mulugeta was invited to go to the Gofa Sefer Church where the preacher was preaching that day on 1 John 1: 6 – 8. That was the day he was converted during the communist era, at the age of 14. This was after the missionaries had left the country and just before the three halls had been taken over.

When we first met Mulugeta, he had been recently married to a lovely spiritual young woman called Alumnish. She like Mulugeta is totally committed to the work of the Lord in Ethiopia. They have a lovely family - Phebe, Moses and Jael. Phebe recently married a very committed young man called Berekit who has a great interest in work among children and teenagers.

When the communist government fell, the believers had a desire to reach out to a new area. They chose a place 90 km west of Addis called Ginchi. The first evangelists who were sent to Ginchi were Asenake and Mulugeta. Already in Ginchi was a brother called Dista who was a school teacher and he was a great help by arranging meetings for Asenake and Mulugeta. He and a sister called Ayn Alem suffered a lot of opposition, but in spite of this they saw the work of God grow to what it is today.

In the first year or two that we were together in Addis, I noticed that Mulugeta's eyesight was very poor. He would try and cross the road unaware of the traffic coming in the opposite direction. When he got to a taxi, he had difficulty in finding the door handle.

I raised the matter with him and it was decided we should visit an eye specialist in Addis. It turned out that Mulugeta had cataracts from an early age and he had just come to accept his limitation. The eye surgeon said that he needed an operation in both eyes, but he was unwilling to operate in Ethiopia in a man as young as Mulugeta.

I then contacted Dr William Harrison from Aberdeen who had worked as a missionary in Zambia where he did some eye surgery. He said he would talk to his old boss Mr Frank Green who was an excellent eye surgeon who decided that he would operate on Mulugeta. He also said that he would put him in his own private clinic and he would not charge the hefty fees for the two operations.

Mulugeta came to Scotland and Mr Green who was a believer first prayed then operated on the first eye. What a day of rejoicing it was when Mr Green pulled off the cotton wool and Mulugeta said, 'I can see!'

After two weeks, Mr Green did the second eye and when we left the clinic Mulugeta was given glasses to wear if needed. Since the operations I have never seen him using them! But Mulugeta has not only improved physical vision, but I have noted over the years that his spiritual vision has become a burden for the whole of Ethiopia.

CHAPTER TWELVE

Development of the Work

In those early days in 1994, a work was being commenced in the countryside and I was made aware of this when I visited a place called Machie. A conference had been arranged there, although I was unaware that it was not instigated by those in assembly fellowship.

I was told that the road to Machie was passable and as a result I rented a four wheel vehicle from Sudan Interior Mission and with a number of other brethren set out from Addis early in the morning. We took the main road from Addis to Ginchi which at that time was rather rough.

From Ginchi we took an even bumpier dry weather road which ascended to the mountain area, travelling along for about 25 km. We then came to a point where a track took us on to very difficult terrain. As I was driving the Land Cruiser, at some points I could only see the sky while the brethren cleared boulders so that the vehicle could continue the journey. We arrived in Chobi about 5pm where at that time there was no assembly.

A man from Chobi said he could give us directions to the track that would ultimately take us to Machie. We negotiated this part of the track, but when we were travelling through some fields suddenly the chassis of the vehicle got stuck in a grass mound and we could not move.

However, after much digging under the vehicle we were able to plough on through the fields till the group arrived at a village called Yibdu. The man from Chobi, who turned out to be a local bandit, tried to encourage the group to travel on as there were other bandits along the track who had planned to rob our group of any valuables that we had.

However, when I arrived at Yibdu I said I was not driving one more kilometre.

As a result we all began to walk down the mountain to Machie. Yibdu is about 9,000 feet and Machie is about 4,000 feet. The single track had to be negotiated in the dark as it was about 7pm. I had a small torch but the batteries died after a short distance. For the rest of the journey I was supported by some brethren to prevent me from falling on the muddy track.

The group finally arrived at the Machie Hall which was filled with believers singing in Oromiffa. We didn't get much sleep that night and we were all wakened up early the next morning to prayer and more singing.

The conference turned out to be a mixed group of believers, some of whom were keen to speak in tongues. This was my first introduction to this area. There is now a large assembly in Machie and I have met many believers who come from there.

If going down the mountain was difficult, the return journey was much more so. When the party arrived back at Yibdu where the Land Cruiser had been parked we all were exhausted, at least I was! Because of losing so much sweat I developed severe cramp in both legs and we had to stop in Chobi to see if we could get some salt to stop the cramp. All that was available in one of the shops was the rough salt given to the cows, but it did the trick and we finally got back to Addis by early evening in what had proved to be a very eventful journey.

I have never been able to return to Machie, but soon there were believers meeting in Yibdu. This was the first assembly in that area, and then an assembly was opened in Chobi. Thus the work of God began to grow in an area where many of the people were either Satan worshippers or were involved in the occult. Many trophies of grace were seen in those early days of assembly work in that area. Those who came to Christ at that time had many strange ideas and those new believers needed much careful teaching.

One brother took me to a big tree in his village. He said that before the Gospel came to them they worshiped at that tree - not that there was anything important about the tree, but that inside the tree there were spirits who had to be satisfied. The local people would bring a sheep or a goat or some other animal to be sacrificed there. That was how things were till the Gospel came to that village.

On one occasion at Yibdu, a brother took me to the place where I could look down the mountain to see where the Machie Hall was. A year or two later I was on the other side of the mountain range and a brother began to point out area after area in the valley in between, where the Gospel had reached and where there were now assemblies of believers meeting. I was told that when the Gospel came to one village it wasn't long till they began to share the Gospel in the next village, and in this way the work of God spread. In this area alone there are now about 160 assemblies with 215 assemblies in the whole of Ethiopia.

Evangelists

Every year when I have been in Ethiopia, they have held an evangelists' conference. Each year that number has been growing from seven at our first conference in 1993 until 2017 when over 200 gathered for a few days of fellowship and teaching. There are now 251 evangelists all supported by their local assemblies.

Many of these brethren live in isolated areas and rarely do they see any of the other evangelists, and as a result they love to come to these conferences. In fact they look forward with great anticipation to the time spent at Ginchi where these conferences are held.

Evangelists' conference 2017

Some travel long distances to get there, but the days spent together mean so much to them that they will not miss these days of Bible study and fellowship. It is also a time when they can share what the Lord is doing in their areas.

There are many practical issues that can be discussed while they are together, and they find others with the same problem as they have.

Asenake

One of the first evangelists among the assemblies was Asenake. When he became an evangelist he didn't want to be called one, but if ever there was a true evangelist it was Asenake. It was on our second trip that the brethren arranged an evangelists' conference. Around seven evangelists attended that first conference when we met in Wilincomi about 80 km west of Addis. In cramped conditions we slept, ate and had Bible teaching in the Wilincomi Hall, but it was a wonderful time of fellowship.

Evangelist Asenake

Asenake was an outstanding personal worker and he could strike up a conversation with anyone about the Bible and about the Gospel. He had been brought up in a village near Ginchi and his father was the local witch doctor. Asenake wanted the power that his father held in the community, but one night he had a dream and in the dream he was told to go over the mountain and visit his brother who had an important book.

He visited his brother who had this book that seemed to be important to him, and when his brother was not in the house Asenake took the book and travelled back to his village. Although he could not understand the central message of this book, he wondered where he could get help.

One day, his uncle invited him to go with him to Addis, and while there he was introduced to the assembly at Gofa Sifir. The brethren told him what the book was all about and in time Asenake trusted the Saviour. He grew in the things of the Lord and he was the first man to see the work of God grow in and around the capital. He had the great joy of seeing the whole family saved apart from his father.

When he first visited Akaki, on the outskirts of Addis, he did not find any believers so he would go behind a hedge and make his bed on the grass for the night. However, soon he met some who showed an interest in the Bible and he had the joy of seeing a small fellowship begun. When we visited Akaki in 1993, the believers were meeting in rented premises on the outskirts of the town and there were around 80 in fellowship. They had begun the assembly a number of years earlier with just three members.

A few years later, a piece of ground became available. There was a dilapidated building on the land which had been used by weavers, and the believers met in this hall for about 17 years.

Original Akaki hall

By this time the assembly had grown and the building had become too small so they decided to build a new hall. With the help of gifts from the United Kingdom this building was commenced in 2011 and finally completed about 2014.

New Akaki hall

I visited the hall in 2015 and I was able to see the completed building. In a small office near the hall there were two charts on one of the walls. When I asked about the charts, I was told that on the first chart the believers had kept a record of assembly members each five years. The numbers had risen from three in 1979 to 1025 in 2015. But the second chart showed that they were a missionary-minded assembly and they had been able to plant six other assemblies in the area. One was about 6 km away, another was 17 km, and another 40 km away. Gradually the work had expanded in four directions.

When the evangelists had the joy of seeing someone trusting the Saviour in a new area, they would commence cottage meetings. There were now four of these in the area and a number of others were being planned. The evangelists are real pioneer workers and when a new work has been established in one area they move on to a new area or to another village.

When I thought of this method it made me think of the work of God in the book of the Acts, and the pattern in Ethiopia was so like that. The Gospel came to Thessalonica and it wasn't long till it was spreading out to Macedonia and Achaia which covers most of modern Greece.

I thought about missionary work during the last 150 years. I noticed that in many places a compound was rented or maybe bought. Then a house was built on it and perhaps a school or a hospital/clinic or both and maybe a Gospel Hall. So the work seemed to revolve round the compound. Local people were employed and often they were the first to believe. Often that was where the missionary stayed all the time that he was in that country. I am aware that this was how things commenced in Ethiopia. When the missionaries left, all these compounds were taken over by the local people.

When we returned in 1993, there were no compounds and no mission stations, and all the work now revolved round the ministry of the evangelists or pioneer workers who just kept moving from place to place, and this is how the work spread.

It is so spiritually healthy to see the work of God in Ethiopia today revolving round these evangelists and the work developing in such an amazing way. In one sense the entrance of communism into Ethiopia was a blessing in disguise, for as a result of persecution the work multiplied and the believers were scattered as in Acts 8. As a result the work spread to areas we had never been in before.

Exodus 1:12, "But the more they afflicted them, the more they multiplied and grew".

This has also been the pattern in the other assemblies in and around Addis Ababa. In some areas of Addis the cost of buying ground is almost impossible, and as a result the assemblies who are in these areas have a very great burden of a heavy rent. Often after the believers have been in one area for some time the landlord will raise the cost of the rent and this forces the believers to move to another site.

In spite of these problems, a number of the evangelists have been reaching out to the north of Addis and already there are five new assemblies in that area. It is so thrilling to see the enthusiasm that these brethren show as they seek to move into new areas with the message of the Gospel.

Fayesa

A number of years ago, I met one of the evangelists and he told me his story. When he was a young man, Fayesa fell off a horse and was badly injured. He was taken to a hospital in Addis, but they said they could not help him. Subsequently, he was taken to a local witch doctor and what he was given affected him mentally. He lived in a darkened room for a year and did not speak to one person. For three months he lived up a tree and had his brother feeding him with earth.

He used to go about the different markets and cause all sorts of problems. When the Gospel came to the next village some believers were praying that Fayesa might go and hear the message of God's love. He eventually did go and was wonderfully converted. The change was immediate and as a result his whole family trusted in Christ, as did a number in his village. He is now a respected evangelist and has seen many coming to Christ.

Evangelist Fayesa

CHAPTER THIRTEEN
Where to Next?

In 2015, the Ethiopian brethren arranged a thanksgiving conference and they sent me an email saying that they were aware of Sheena's [Mum's] ill health and if I wasn't able to come they would understand. However at that time, Sheena's health wasn't too bad and she was happy for me to go to Ethiopia for a month.

As I attended that conference and thought over what had happened since 1991, I must confess tears were shed, and I was so glad Sheena felt well enough for me to be there. I deeply appreciated that a number of sisters locally were able to visit Sheena regularly while I was away, and that helped immensely.

25th conference at Ginchi

About 450 believers had been invited from different churches, but I think some who had not been invited also came to the conference. We had a wonderful day at Ginchi.

The conference was divided to review three aspects of the service of God over 60 years.

1. Firstly, a report was to be given to look back to the beginning of the assembly work from 1952 to 1978, and I was given the task of delivering this account.

50th anniversary conference at Batie

Earlier, John Flynn had been able to be in Ethiopia in 2002 when a special conference was arranged in Addis and in Batie. One of the speakers at Batie was a brother called Hossain who had been converted while attending school in Batie many years earlier. We were so glad that John Flynn, although quite unwell, had been able to attend the conference, and just a few months later he was called home to heaven.

Originally a work for the Lord in Ethiopia was begun in 1952 by John and Marty Flynn.

When others went to Ethiopia to help, there was some development when the Millikens went to Dubtie in the '60s and further development in 1971 when the McQuoids went to the capital to begin another new work. Around the same time the Cunninghams went to Dagan to begin a fourth new work.

2. Then there was an account of what God had done during the 25 years since 1990 in the area west of Addis, initially at Ginchi and then moving out to the countryside. A number of local evangelists gave these accounts.

3. Finally, there was an account of what the brethren were burdened about for the future in their desire to move out to new areas that had not yet been reached.

In 1991, there was a significant development of the work after the fall of communism, when those living in the capital had a burden for another outreach in the west of Addis at Ginchi and further afield.

First hall at Ginchi

In a town called Wilincomi about 80 km from Addis there was a small assembly. They had recently bought a piece of ground and were meeting in a small hall which in time proved to be too small. So they decided to build a larger hall behind the existing one, and this new hall is now filled to capacity on a Sunday.

About 15 km further west, there is a town called Ginchi. When this was first visited in 1993, the believers had bought a small piece of ground on which was a small hall where a small group of believers worshipped, but there was much persecution.

After a short time, the believers were given a larger piece of ground on which a new hall was built, and where a growing number of believers were able to meet. At that time a kindergarten was commenced and soon the assembly grew. The animosity in the town gradually subsided.

But the work was spreading to new areas all the time. In 2012 when I arrived at a town called Geldu, a new hall had just been opened. I met a brother called Kitima and his wife standing outside the new hall. He asked me if I remembered the year 2000. I said I did, and remembered at that time there was only Kitima and his wife and another brother meeting together.

Sunday morning at Geldu

They met in a very small hall about 3 metres square and they were often disturbed by stones being thrown onto the roof. It was in that year that Kitima's wife developed shingles near her eye, and sadly she lost the sight of one eye. A few years later, she was called home to heaven. Kitima invited me into the new hall where about 300 people were gathered, many of them new believers. Added to that they had commenced another outreach work called Geldu Number 2 where there were over 40 baptised believers and I was asked to preach in that hall that morning.

In another town called Shikutey the work was just starting around the year 2000. A piece of ground with a hall on it was purchased, and that work has now grown to a large assembly. The surrounding areas have also been evangelised and there is now a new assembly on the outskirts of the town and in a number of areas around the town of Shikutey.

In Shikutey there lived one of the first evangelists called Gellassa. He told me that around the year 2006 he was burdened about reaching a place called Kachisi where he felt the desire to evangelise that area. It was discovered later that a brother called Dhaba, who now helps Mulugeta in the office, had been meeting with six sisters and seeking to teach them the Word of God.

Evangelist Gellassa

The distance from Gellassa's village to Kachisi was about 12-14 hours by horseback, and when Gellassa first went there he was beaten up and told never to return. However, he did go back and gradually a number of assemblies were commenced. I have been able to visit three of these country assemblies in Ginda Birit itself, in Tenyee and Fito. There are now eight assemblies in this area.

A new town near Kachisi has recently been built and a new assembly called Abuna has been formed where there are about 50 believers in fellowship.

Asgorie

In 1994, we visited a village called Asgorie about 20 km further on than Ginchi. At that time, meetings had been stopped and the believers were meeting in a home. The reason was that two bandits had been causing real fear in the village – their names were Light and Love! For some incident 'Love' was put in prison and while there he was converted. He is now one of the elders in that village assembly. The numbers have grown to such a degree that after two extensions the brethren have decided to build a new hall.

Believers in the hall at Asgorie

Kora

When I first visited Kora, the believers were meeting in one of the local homes with about 15 in fellowship. One of the elders called Geleta has seen that assembly grow to what it is today. One Sunday over coffee I asked him how he was saved. He said that a number of years earlier, his brother had gone to Addis and been converted.

He came back to Kora and began to witness to Geleta, but he was not interested for he liked to drink the local beer. However, after 15 years Geleta was converted. When the local priest heard of this, he told the people to maim Geleta so that he could no longer farm. In spite of all this opposition the work has grown and that assembly has extended their hall twice, once lengthways and then sideways.

Hall at Kora

Bali

Not too long ago, some farmers moved from the Chobi area to another area called Bali. This is a very strongly Islamic area, but in spite of this, in 2015 a new work for God began to grow. The brethren took me to a central town and they said that rather than me going into the area, some of the brethren would come out to have a meeting with me.

Some walked 9 hours to get the bus and some walked 5 hours to get the same bus, About 18 brethren came to have the meeting with me, and it was so encouraging to see them. They said that as a result of them going to this area there were now five fellowships, and they had been greatly encouraged to see this growth. In a report given in October 2017, one of the evangelists said that five Muslims had been converted.

Bali elders and evangelists

Kaffa

Another new work that commenced in 2016 is in the region called Kaffa. This is the province that Mulugeta comes from. Part of it has been well evangelised by the Sudan Interior Mission, but the area the brethren have moved into is totally unevangelised. There are around 400 witchdoctors in this region who control the people. The place where we went was Adiyo, in Kaffa province, in a very difficult part of the country, with a very difficult road to negotiate. Four young believers from Addis had gone ahead of us and had children's meetings for about four days with around 30 children coming to hear from the Bible for the first time.

Children at Adiyo

While we were there we met the first fruits of the work. In the village was a man who was an alcoholic and he was wonderfully converted. There are now six believers in this new work and we pray that the Lord will add to their number. When I visited Ethiopia in October 2017, I discovered that there are now forty believers in Adiyo, for which we praise the Lord.

New converts at Adiyo

Jimma

The main large town nearest Adiyo is Jimma. For some time the brethren were thinking about starting a new work here. The initial reason was that there is a fairly big university there which accepts students from all over Ethiopia. Many of our students come from the Chobi area who speak mainly Oromiffa, well away from home and parents who often had great difficulty contacting them unless at holiday time.

The journey to Jimma is on a good tarmac road. We initially made this journey with a view to seeing some of the students, just to be there to encourage them in their Christian life.

At that time, we were also able to see Mulugeta's mother who had come from her home to meet us as she lives in this area. We had a lovely time of fellowship with the students and this began regular visits to Jimma.

Only in 2015 the work began to make progress. The brethren were able to purchase a piece of ground on which there was a building and this is where the believers are now meeting. The brethren feel that this might be the beginning of more work in other parts nearby. One or two believers are now lecturers at the university in Jimma so this will also be a help. When we were there in 2017, we met in two of their homes.

Students at Jimma University

CHAPTER FOURTEEN

Children's Work

When the missionaries were in Ethiopia from 1952 to 1978, they had Sunday Schools in Batie, Dagan and Addis, but these did not function during the communist era.

Around 1994, God raised up among the assemblies a young man called Digaffe who was a member of the assembly in Akaki. He had a particular burden for work among children, so when he became an evangelist he asked the assembly at Akaki to commend him to be involved in children's work.

He then set about encouraging all the existing assemblies in and around the capital and subsequently further afield to set up Sunday Schools. After a year or two, he invited Sheena and me to attend a gathering for children in the Akaki hall on a Saturday morning. When we arrived at the hall it was filled with about 500 children from Sunday Schools in different parts of Addis.

The whole day was spent with the children. During the break, the sisters provided lunch for the children. Digaffe was so pleased with the response that he said to me that it would be wonderful if they could have more time with the children and for a longer period. This conversation prompted me to begin discussing with a number of brethren the possibility of a centre where a camp site could be arranged.

The big question was where could a site be found for this kind of work? But God had been at work ahead of this conversation as the brethren in Ginchi had applied for a larger piece of ground to commence not only the building of a hall but also to commence a kindergarten for the children in Ginchi. Amazingly, this ground was given by the communist government with no charge although there had been some dispute among the officials about granting this ground to an evangelical group.

Plans had been drawn up and had been approved by the government, and when I and some other brethren went to Ginchi and proposed setting up a camp site there I was shown their plans - these were exactly the kind of plans that I had formulated in my own mind.

Since these plans had been approved by the government, the site was enclosed by a fence and work was started immediately. The first block for sleeping quarters was to be commenced and a camp was to be arranged for the following year.

When Sheena and I went to see the site in the January of the following year, the first building was still not completed, but the brethren were still keen for the camp to be held. They said that they could hire a tent where the boys could sleep, and the girls originally were to be housed with believers in the town.

First camp at Ginchi

However, after some discussion it was decided that the girls would sleep in the existing hall which would also be used for the meetings. I felt that because of the limited accommodation that the numbers should be limited to 40, but when all the children arrived there were almost 60. In spite of this, the camp was a complete success.

Each year, new buildings were erected until finally there were six dorms, a kitchen, dining hall and by this time a large meeting hall. The site was divided into two, and the second part was used for all kinds of athletic activities.

God had prepared me for this new work, as during the years when I was out of Ethiopia in the UK I had been invited to over 40 camps in 28 years. Therefore, I had a good idea of what was needed for Ethiopia. Mulugeta's brother-in-law Teddy was a great help in putting up all these dorms and building the excellent conference hall which is now still being used widely.

The football contests were very popular (as usual!) and although the ground was quite uneven, when the boys played, one would have thought it was a World Cup game! The camp was finally able to take 250 children and this has proved to be such a blessing for so many. Years later, I would often be greeted by a young man or a young woman who had been at camp years earlier, and they would say that camp was the time when they took Christianity seriously.

Many of the present camp leaders who are either in work among children or teenagers were originally spoken to at camp. One brother called Solomon, who was quite a quiet leader, in later years felt an exercise along with his wife to be involved in evangelism in a province called Somalia on the border of Ethiopia with Somalia. This area is a very strongly Muslim area and a very difficult area to work in.

Solomon and his wife in Somalia

About the year 2010, some of the brethren spoke to me about a difficulty with the camp. Their concern was that the Sunday Schools had now grown, and most of them in and around the capital had over 200, but each assembly was only allowed to send 25 children to camp. Some children never attended and they felt another solution had to be found.

When they were asked what alternative they could suggest, they felt that in place of the camp they could have a Daily Vocational Bible School in each assembly which all the children could attend. The first year when this happened was a great success. In the countryside where the children spoke the Oromiffa language, 1,000 children were enrolled during that week.

At the end of the week, a bus trip was organised, when six buses took the children to a water purifying plant and then on to a site where a lovely lunch had been provided for them. This has proved to be a great success and has been continued for some years.

In 2015, I had a meeting with ex-campers and leaders and we had a great day together. Most of the testimonies that were given by the young folk showed the important place that the camp work had had in their lives. Many of those present spoke of how the Lord had clearly spoken to them about total commitment of their lives to Him.

Those who were camp leaders said that camp gave them the new desire to be engaged in work among children themselves. All without exception are now engaged in either Sunday School work or work among teenagers. Some of them said it was at camp that they met their husbands or wives. Camp had proved such a blessing to many.

All of them said that they would like to see the camp recommenced. I suggested that the only way that I felt that this could be done was for each assembly individually to organise a week totally for their own Sunday School. It has been decided that camp work will recommence in January 2018.

Literature

In 2012, I had a conversation with Sam Balmer who runs the Postal Bible School. He told me that they were interested in translating their booklets for the children into Amharic.

This was finally completed in 2016 and a large assignment was sent to Ethiopia for distribution. They hope that soon the same books will be translated into the Oromo language and used in the countryside. In Africa they call it Bible Education Services or BES. These books have been printed by Revival Movement, a company in Northern Ireland, which does a wonderful work for countries outside of the United Kingdom.

In 2017, Sam Balmer and Stephen Gilham visited Ethiopia and during their stay we had two seminars when a large number of leaders of children's work gathered for training on how to use the BES books.

The assemblies also had a special seminar when 28 leaders came from all over Ethiopia for a week's training. They then went back to their own areas and each passed on this training to ten Sunday School teachers. These Sunday School teachers would each try and enrol 40 new children for their Sunday Schools - already they have reached over 7,500 new children.

Sunday School leaders

CHAPTER FIFTEEN

Transport

For a long number of years, many of the villages in the countryside were isolated. Initially, we would take a Land Cruiser as far as we could go and then travel either on foot or on horseback. As these villages were about 10,000 feet above sea level the **best option** was the horse! The only problem was that the horses had wooden saddles, and after 5 hours in the saddle you really knew you had been riding a horse.

Horse riding to Chobi

Fairly recently the government has been putting dry weather roads into these villages, so it has been a bit easier to reach them by Land Cruiser. For some years the brethren had a 1989 Toyota Land Cruiser which has covered over 700,000 km so it is past its sell by date!

1989 Toyota Land Cruiser

However, through the kindness of a dear brother the brethren were able to buy another Toyota Land Cruiser sourced in Italy. It runs so smoothly and is so comfortable. I wondered if they should sell the older vehicle but they felt they should keep it for the difficult countryside roads and use the new vehicle for the tarmac roads - this was a wise decision.

2000 Toyota Land Cruiser

On many occasions, we got stuck in the mud on these dry weather roads and we had to be pulled out of ditches etc. in order to continue on our journey. We also had many punctures on these roads and the tyres didn't last all that long. Sometimes the suspension broke and that meant the vehicle had to be taken back to Addis.

Motorcycles

In 2015, in Scotland I showed a slide with one of the evangelists sitting on a motorcycle that belonged to someone else. In the countryside there are four mature evangelists who have the responsibility of helping other younger evangelists in their area. If some problem arises, these evangelists can call on one of the four to come and help them. At the moment, it can take quite a time for these mature evangelists to travel elsewhere to give help, and it was felt that a motorcycle might be the answer.

One brother who saw this picture in the United Kingdom asked how much it would cost to buy one motorcycle. I had no idea so we asked Mulugeta - he thought that you could buy one for about £3000. The brother then said that he had £3000 which he would send with me the next time I was in Ethiopia. When I arrived in Addis in June 2016, I told the brethren that I had £3000 to buy a motorcycle. But they were not too happy about this, and they felt that we should wait till we had enough money to buy four.

We then decided to visit the market where motorcycles were sold. The first place that we went to was selling Chinese motorcycles, but they seemed to be of a poor quality, so we moved on.

At the next shop we visited, they were selling what looked like very substantial motorcycles called Hero. I had never heard of Hero so I told the salesman that I would return later. I immediately went on to the internet to find out about this company to discover that this company was the biggest manufacturer of motorcycles in the world. The managing director had worked with Honda and he then had set up a company in India called Hero. We returned to the shop and I asked the salesman just out of interest what would be the cost of four motorcycles. He saw his boss and then he came back and said we could have four motorcycles for £3000!

We were delighted with this news and so we bought the four motorcycles. I called for the four evangelists to come to Addis. You can just picture their faces when they saw the motorcycles - but there was a major problem - none of the evangelists had a driver's licence.

One of the brethren assured me that he could ride a motorcycle, but we assured them all that none of the motorcycles were leaving the office until they all had their licence! Amazingly when I arrived six months later they all had their licences! These motorcycles will be a great blessing to the work of the Lord in Ethiopia.

One of the evangelists with a Hero motorcycle

On one occasion, I was invited to an assembly that I had never visited before called Bikay. The evangelist, Tadisa, who invited me said he was sad that I had travelled elsewhere but had never visited them. So I asked him how far it was to his village. He said if we took our Land Cruiser to a spot near Ginchi he would ensure that horses were there and by horse it would take about one to one and a half hours to complete the journey.

We took the vehicle to the given spot, and sure enough the horses were there for us to complete our journey. The path that we took was steeper than anything I had ever encountered on any part of the countryside.

After five hours we were still on our journey to Bikay! However, when we arrived at our destination it almost seemed that the whole village had turned out to see us. I discovered afterwards that they had never seen a white man before in that village.

When I asked Tadisa why he had told me the wrong journey time, he said that he was afraid that if he had told me the truth I might never have made the journey! However, we had our first conference there and a large number turned up. I felt that the journey was worthwhile.

Horse riding to Bikay

In 2017 we had an excellent conference in another assembly called Bikay No.2 which is on the outskirts of Bikay and the hall was filled each day of the conference. It is so encouraging to see the way that the doors are opening up even when there is another assembly in the same village.

CHAPTER SIXTEEN

Chobi Bible School

Somewhere else that the work of God has grown is in a place called Chobi. When I passed through Chobi in 1993 there was no assembly there. But the message of the Gospel soon reached Chobi and an assembly was formed. There are now three other assemblies in the town of Chobi.

As it was a centre for the surrounding areas, it was decided to have a conference there. At the first conference I attended there were about 750 believers coming from four different directions. It was lovely to see and hear the believers congregating from other areas, for as they travelled to the conference they sang hymns - you could hear them before you saw them. Many of them had travelled at least three to four hours on very rugged terrain.

A few years later, the number at the conference had grown to over 3,000. These believers had come over difficult mountain paths to sit on the grass, as there was no hall big enough, to listen to the Gospel and to listen to Bible teaching.

On one occasion as I was speaking, after about one and a half hours by interpretation as I cannot speak in Oromiffa, I was about to close my Bible when a brother, in the front row said, 'Go on brother!' These believers have been saved from Satan worship and witchcraft and Bible teaching now means so much to them. Many of them will return home in the dark to their villages and they will feel that travelling to the conference was well worth the journey. Their enthusiasm and commitment is quite a challenge to those in the west.

Conference at Chobi

Bible School

In order that elders and evangelists could be taught in a consecutive way a Bible School was commenced at Chobi in 1987. It started in a very small way as they had no water and no electricity, and the accommodation was just two rooms where the brethren could sleep and eat and study.

It was a self supporting Bible School and those attending had to come for six weeks at the beginning of each year for a period of three years. The assembly that they came from was responsible to provide their food for the six weeks when they were at the Bible School.

In the Bible School they are taught the doctrine of God, the doctrine of Christ, the doctrine of the Holy Spirit, the message of the Gospel and so on. They also do an overview of the Old and New Testaments, a study of some of the major prophets and minor prophets, and studies in the New Testament books as well. After they have completed the three years' study they are given a diploma certificate, and I have attended many of these special occasions.

On the day the brethren are being given their diplomas, some of the elders from the brother's own assembly would attend, and some would have walked for about six hours to get there.

There are some able teachers from in and around Addis and one of them would go and give teaching on his subject at the Bible School for a week, and then he would be replaced by another brother from the capital on the next week and so on.

Normally there would be about 35 attending, but in 2017 there were over 60 present. How we thank God for the interest that is being shown for the Bible School.

A building has now been put up where the teaching takes place, and dorms can now cater for about 35 brethren. This has proved a real blessing for the assemblies as they are teaching a first generation church. Most of these brethren come from villages where they once practised the worship of pieces of wood or stone.

They were normally in fear of the witch doctor who had great influence in the village where they lived. Stories were told of the witch doctor casting a spell on ground to prevent any harvest from it, and that often would come to pass.

When some of the people trusted in Christ, they would go round the witch doctor's house and pray that either he would believe in Christ or he would move to another area.

2017 Bible School at Chobi

Graduation day at Chobi

CHAPTER SEVENTEEN

Development in Wallo Province

The work of evangelism in Wallo province at Batie and Dagan never really developed to the same degree as in other parts because these two areas were strongly Islamic. They had the joy of seeing some trusting in Christ at Batie and Dagan, but believers were unable to get work and so they usually had to move to other towns.

A number of projects were tried in Batie, for example a chicken farm but because food for the chickens was so expensive that effort soon came to a halt. They thought of developing a kindergarten, but that never seemed to get off the ground.

The assemblies had for some time been working with a para-church group called *Compassion* based in USA but with an office in England. At this time six assemblies were benefitting from it. Their motto is threefold. The work must be 'Christ centred', 'Church focussed' and 'Child based'. *Compassion* will help children who are very poor or who are orphans. They have a strict code of acceptance before they will register the children.

Once registered, *Compassion* will help children from kindergarten through to university. The believers at Batie felt that this might have been helpful for them, and so they applied to *Compassion* to commence a work there. *Compassion* normally requires a church to be a certain size before they will consider their application, but because this was in an Islamic area they said they would accept Batie as they were.

The number of children now being helped at Batie is 236. When I visited the assembly there, I was shown the statistics of the children being helped. There are now 203 children from a Muslim background, 26 from an Orthodox background and 7 from a Protestant background.

On a recent visit to Batie, I found a good spirit among the believers. They had just built new toilets for the children in the *Compassion* project, and on the Sunday the children sang for us some choruses. It was so encouraging to see many of the guardians of the children at the service.

Compassion needed an accountant to look after the financial matters. One of the original believers at Batie had a daughter, a believer, who was an accountant and she was chosen for this job.

A social worker was also required for this project and a brother called Imam was appointed. Imam was a Muslim who had been converted some years earlier at Batie. He could not find work there so he had to travel a considerable distance to another village where he trained as a social worker. He now goes round all the parents of these children and it provides him with a great opportunity to present the message of the Gospel.

It was a great joy to see those Muslim children singing about the Saviour, and doing this in front of their guardians who had come to hear them. It was also wonderful that they were hearing the preaching of the Gospel, something that had never happened before. In Dagan in the 1970s there were those Muslims who came and told us that they believed the message of the Gospel to be true, but they were afraid that they would be cut off from the rest of the village if they were converted and baptised.

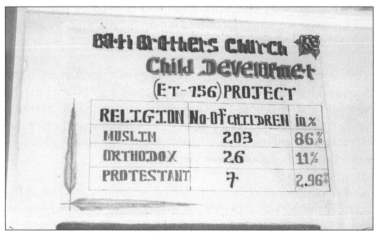

RELIGION	No Of children	in %
MUSLIM	203	86%
ORTHODOX	26	11%
PROTESTANT	7	2.96%

Statistics of children at Batie supported by Compassion

Another great encouragement was the conversion of a man called Hassan*[name changed]. This man lived in a village a good distance away from the main road which was 100% Islamic. Hassan's parents were keen for him to become a Muslim teacher so they sent him to a Koranic school where he studied the Koran for 13 years.

One of his Muslim teachers had an Arabic Bible and he would tear pages out of it to give to his students to be used as a bookmark. Hassan was given Genesis 12 and he began to read all about Abraham. He asked the Muslim teacher's son to get the rest of the book and he began to read this new book which was different from the Koran.

At the same time, Hassan used to listen to Radio Voice of America in Arabic to improve his Arabic as his own language was Oromiffa. One night as he turned on his radio he heard Arabic, but this time it was the Gospel being beamed in from Lebanon. Sometime later while listening to his radio he heard the Gospel again, but this time it was in Oromiffa, his own language, and it was coming from Far East Broadcasting Association in the Seychelles.

Hassan was so keen to learn more about this message that he went to the Orthodox Church. But he was told that he was maybe just interested in stealing from the church and he was sent away. One day Hassan took ill and he went to his local clinic. That morning one of the helpers at the clinic was a Christian from the Batie assembly and he was singing a hymn.

Hassan went up to him and asked if he knew anything about the book he had in his hand. He was told to wait till the end of the clinic. The brother who was an energetic believer poured into his ears the Gospel, and suggested he come down to the hall in Batie to speak to the evangelist. When Hassan arrived at the hall the local evangelist had the great joy of leading him to trust in the Saviour.

Some years later, Hassan was baptised in the local church. At present, he is now involved in steadily seeking to reach other Muslims with the Gospel, and in the south of the country they have seen some Muslims coming to Christ.

Kamisay

About 300 km from Addis is a town called Kamisay. This town has a large teaching mosque from which they send out Muslims to teach Islam to the people in the area. The town is about 98% Islamic with 19 mosques in it. Some years ago a number of believers from the Chobi area applied for jobs mainly in the Agriculture College as the language spoken in Kamisay is Oromiffa.

They were soon eager to see an assembly formed, and a piece of ground was bought and a hall was built. Initially this assembly was quite small but gradually it has increased in size, so that now there are quite a number of believers in fellowship. They also have two outreaches in the vicinity and believers are meeting in the three places.

A while ago, some young men burned down three evangelical buildings in the town, but the assembly hall escaped. A young man called Chalchisa worked as an evangelist in this area, but recently he has moved to Addis where he is involved in evangelism on the outskirts of that town. Already there are five fellowships seeking to reach the people in the area north of Addis.

Addis development

Addis Ababa, the capital of Ethiopia, has grown in the last ten years at a phenomenal rate. The government has embarked on a policy of demolishing large areas of the city where the houses are single storey and normally made of mud and corrugated sheeting, most without plans. These have been replaced by what the locals call condominiums, usually five storeys tall.

When a gentleman from India revisited Addis recently, one of the Ethiopians said to him that Addis had expanded. To this the Indian replied, 'Addis has not expanded, it has exploded.' With all this expansion in this large city there are many opportunities for evangelism in these new areas.

Gofa Sifir, Saris and Akaki are some of the areas in greater Addis where they not only have a large assembly, but they have the desire to reach out to new areas around the capital.

Teaching mosque at Kamisay

Young believers at Kamisay

CHAPTER EIGHTEEN

Literature Work

Another task that I have been engaged in is the translation of books from English to Amharic and Oromiffa. It all began when I spoke to the brethren about producing a concordance in Amharic. When they asked me what was the meaning of the word "concordance" I was not sure what to say! But when they asked me what the book was used for, they decided that they would call their book 'The words that you get out of the Bible'.

The first concordance that was produced was similar to the Crudens concordance with simply the word and the references, but nothing else. At that time in 1999 there were 5,000 copies printed and we thought that these would last for a long time. However, the sales were so good that the brethren felt that there should be another printing as early as 2001. By this time I felt that I should try to produce an encyclopaedic concordance taken from an English Study Bible.

This provided a lot more information about each word, but this task was much greater and involved months of scrutiny of each entry. It was rather tedious but there were times of light relief. On one occasion I came across the entry of 'eagle'. The definition in English was 'a bird of prey' but when it was translated into Amharic it was 'a bird who prays'!

Another entry on Jonah had reference to the fact that Jonah was swallowed by a whale. But when it was translated into Amharic a letter was omitted which made it read that Jonah 'swallowed a whale'! All these books have been printed locally in Ethiopia, and this one was sold for about 70 pence for a book containing about 370 pages.

Concordances in Amharic and Oromiffa

Other books have been translated over the years, such as 'New Testament Church Principles' by A.J. Clark, 'The Last Times' by John Campbell, 'Knowing and Doing' by John McQuoid, and most recently the five books produced by *Precious Seed* on an 'Overview of the New Testament'.

Before any of these books can be translated, I had to edit them to remove or change words that would be difficult to translate into Amharic and that involved many weeks of work. I also had to remove idiomatic phrases that would be impossible to translate into another language and into another culture. Over the past 25 years many booklets have also been translated, which have been a great blessing to the local believers.

As I look back over the last 25 years, I praise God for the way that the local evangelists and believers have taken more and more responsibility themselves. I have been so thankful for the maturity I have seen among the believers – it has been so encouraging.

Discipleship Course

About seven years ago, Mulugeta Ashagre went to Kenya where a discipleship course from America was being run. Mulugeta had to attend one week every four months and as there were 10 modules the course took three years to complete. Every module had a book with about 300 pages. A part of the 1st book was covered during the week in Kenya, and the rest would be completed when Mulugeta returned home.

An important stipulation was that when the 5th module was reached, Mulugeta would have to commence a new group of his own with no less than five believers, and he would work with them while completing the course in Kenya.

Mulugeta completed the course and graduated about 4 years ago. By that time the believers who had commenced the course were now on their 5th module - and they themselves had to commence a new course with at least five new believers. Some of the subjects covered in these ten modules are as follows -

1. Finishing the great commission of Matt. 28:18-20
2. Church planting
3. How to learn Bible study methods and sermon preparation
4. How to teach evangelism and discipleship training
5. Developing leaders and beginning discipleship training
6. How to teach the entire Bible to an entire church
7. How to teach Bible doctrines to an entire church.

In 2016, the first group of believers graduated, and there were 63 of them. In 2017, they are expecting over 100 to graduate. These courses have produced maturity among the believers and this has been a great help especially in the countryside. The assemblies photocopy all the books then print them and finally bind them so that takes a lot of time and money. Everyone who is on the course will buy the books for each module, so there is quite a commitment when one starts the course to see it through to the end.

Discipleship group

CHAPTER NINETEEN
Sheena's Illness and Homecall

It would be impossible to overestimate the tremendous help and support that Sheena gave me both in Ethiopia and back home in Scotland as we worked closely together for the Lord for 49 years of our 54 years marriage.

Little did either of us know what was involved when we said on our wedding day, 'I will'. But during all those years, I deeply valued a great encourager whom I could talk with and pray with about our service for the Lord.

Sheena and I were together when we went to Ethiopia in 1969. We were there for ten years and her input in so many different ways was as important as mine. She not only worked in the maternity clinic, but she was a great help to the local women.

Sheena showing care to a very poor family with HIV

It was during this time that Sheena's parents visited us and saw the sterling work their daughter was involved in. The letters to us after they returned home were so different from the ones before they came to Ethiopia.

From 1993 to 2012, Sheena joined me for three months every year as we travelled widely in Bible teaching, and when possible Sheena was at my side.

Almost always when Mulugeta and I were out of Addis, one of our senior leaders called Groom looked after Sheena and took her to the place where he was preaching that day. Sheena always said that Groom always gave an excellent message and she often said that she felt he was one of our ablest evangelists. When the memorial service was held, it was Groom who gave the excellent appreciation of her ministry. Groom often took Sheena to many poor people around Gofa Sifir and Sheena was able to give them some practical help. Groom was a great help to Sheena in so many different ways.

Some years ago, she was going into the centre of Addis by taxi, and while standing waiting for it a lady called Alumnish stopped to give her a lift into town. This lady has spent a lot of her time setting up schools for children who are too poor to go to the local schools. She looks after them in so many different ways and we were able to support one of her girls from kindergarten to university.

Alumnish and Sheena with the girl who graduated

In 2012, Sheena began to be quite breathless when she walked only a short distance. She attended the cardiac specialist in Ayr hospital and after having had an angiogram he told her that she had a blockage in the heart and it was impossible to put in a stent in that place. Sheena was then transferred to the Golden Jubilee Hospital where a Mr Fraser Sutherland operated on her. She had a heart bypass operation and the effect was almost immediate. She made an excellent recovery and later in 2013 we were able to have a holiday in Wales.

It was during that holiday that Sheena kept saying she had a real discomfort in her lower abdomen. When we returned from holiday she visited one of our GPs in Tarbolton and he referred her to Ayr Hospital. She was admitted to hospital and was under a Dr Ali who began to do a number of tests, as he was perplexed as to what was causing the pain.

After he did a laparoscopy and took some specimens, it was discovered that Sheena had peritoneal cancer. It had taken Dr Ali some time to discover this, as peritoneal cancer is very rare in women.

We were then sent to the Beatson Centre in Glasgow where we saw Dr Sadozie the oncologist. He said right away that he felt that chemotherapy should be commenced, and although they could not cure the disease they would try and control it. During the first course of treatment which lasted about 6 months, Sheena had some severe side effects from the treatment, but she bore it bravely.

She had a break for a time, but when the cancer marker went up again Dr Sadozie felt that she should have a second course of chemotherapy. This time the side effects were more severe than before, and yet in a wonderful way Sheena bore it with such grace.

Many a time when she would rise in the morning, she would say, 'God has blessed me with another day' and during this time she just thought of a day at a time. I must say that because of the way she treated her illness she was a lesson to those of us who watched her. During this time, the family were so supportive with their phone calls and often with their visits.

She carried on with this treatment and finally she had a third course of chemotherapy which initially was a milder version, but when it did not work effectively Dr Sadozie put her back on to her previous treatment.

In October 2015, when we went to see Dr Sadozie he said that the cancer marker had gone higher than before, and suggested a further course of chemotherapy. Sheena telephoned him three days later and said that she and the family had discussed the matter and she had decided to take no more chemotherapy. She told him that if she was given another six months of chemotherapy she would have no quality of life. The treatment might give her a few more months, but she said she wanted quality of life and not quantity.

She told Dr Sadozie that she knew where she was going and that she wasn't afraid to die. He said he admired her faith. She did have a reasonable quality of life and some of the family spent Christmas with us which was so precious.

Just the day before Sheena was called Home she became unwell and no amount of medicine seemed to have any effect. She wakened me about 3.30am on that day and asked me to pray for her, as in her own words she believed she was going home to heaven. It was not an easy thing to do, but three hours later after she got out of bed she fell into my arms and was at home in heaven.

I was so thankful that Jane our daughter and Norman our son were with me to give such needed support, and Crawford was just a phone call away.

The funeral was held in the Church of Scotland as our hall would have been too small for the large company which gathered to support us in our grief. John McQuoid, with whom we had spent a long time in Ethiopia, chaired the service.

William Fulton spoke on behalf of the assembly at Tarbolton, Crawford our oldest child spoke on behalf of the family. When Mulugeta had heard that Sheena [or 'Mum' as he called her] had passed away, he decided he must come for the funeral and he spoke on behalf of the believers in Ethiopia.

Ian Steele from Glenburn gave the message from the Scriptures and Ian Wallace spoke at the graveside. There had been some snow that day and it was bitterly cold, but as far as Sheena was concerned she was now at home with the Lord.

I felt I could not go to Ethiopia in the early part of the year as we normally had done, but I decided to go in June for two months. The first Sunday that I was there the believers had a memorial service for Sheena in Addis. A large company came from all over Ethiopia to show how much Sheena had meant to them.

There was one incident that really touched my heart. I had been invited to Batie to speak one Sunday and I must confess I thought nothing about it. I gave the message and afterwards Gidifawo, one of the elders, stood up and began to speak of all the history of Sheena's ministry in their area. At the end he then said they wanted to give me three gifts.

These gifts were all wrapped up and when I received the first gift it felt like a picture. I thought it may have been be a scene in Ethiopia. The second felt like a scroll, and the third gift was from Gidifawo's wife - it was a large piece of cloth that you put on if it is cold. We then went and had a meal and then someone suggested that I had a look at the gifts.

Up until then I had no inkling as to what they were, but when I took off the paper I must confess I could not contain myself. On the right hand side was a picture of Sheena and on the left was 2 Timothy 4:7 in English and Amharic. The scroll also had her photo along with **Hebrews 6:10, "For God is not unrighteous to forget your work and labour of love, which ye have shewed toward his name, in that ye have ministered to the saints and do minister".**

Gift from the believers at Batie

CHAPTER TWENTY

Appreciation

During my visit to Ethiopia in 2017, on my last Sunday I was invited to speak at a town called Holeta outside of Addis on the road to Ginchi. This is a completely new work and when I got to the hall it was filled to capacity and there was an overflow outside. It is so thrilling to see the growth of the church first hand, and I felt that the Lord was speaking to some during that Sunday.

On my road back to Addis I said to Mulugeta that I needed to go to one of the hotels as the internet connection elsewhere was very poor, so he dropped me off and said he had something to do at home.

After I had got all my emails downloaded I felt that Mulugeta was slow in returning. However, he did come back and he said that Groom, one of the evangelists, had some questions to ask me, and Mulugeta would drop me off at Gofa Sifir hall.

So we proceeded to the hall and as I walked into the hall suddenly I discovered that in the hall was a large number of people. Completely unknown to me, a special meeting had been arranged and when I stepped into the hall they all began to sing 'Happy Birthday'! It was a bit ahead of the date, but I was deeply touched by this gesture as they had come to celebrate my 80th birthday.

But added to that, representatives from all over Ethiopia had come to Addis to celebrate 50 years spent in the work of the Lord. It was humbling to receive many gifts from believers from all over Ethiopia - some had travelled many kilometres to be there.

I feel that the most touching moment was when I was given a plaque celebrating what we had put into the work of God in Ethiopia, and my only regret was that Sheena was not there to share in this moment. This work, as I have thought it over many times since, could never have been accomplished apart from the amazing support in prayer and in a practical way by so many over these 50 years.

It has been an honour to have served with our Ethiopian brethren over many years and we thank God for what He has accomplished during this time. Without the ministry of the Holy Spirit in people's lives nothing would have been accomplished. Truly what we have seen has been 'a work of God in Ethiopia'.

MR. ROBERT CRAWFORD REVIE

WE ARE HIGHLY INDEBTED TO YOU WITH APPRECIATION AND ACKNOWLEDGEMENT FOR YOUR LONG AND FRUITFUL SERVICE IN THE WORK OF GOD'S KINGDOM IN ETHIOPIA AND WANT TO SAY "HAPPY 50TH YEAR IN YOUR SPIRITUAL MINISTRY" AND ALSO "HAPPY BIRTH DAY TO YOU!" IN THE SPECIAL OCCASION THAT YOU CELEBRATE YOUR 80TH BIRTHDAY.

AS THE ETHIOPIAN BRETHREN CHURCH COMMUNITY, WE HAVE A SPECIAL AND LONG LASTING PLACE IN OUR HEART FOR YOU FOR ALL YOU HAVE DONE TO MOVE THIS CHURCH TO WHERE IT IS NOW.

Mulugeta Ashagre
General Secretary and, Representative of the Ethiopian Brethren Churches.

Tekola Goshime
Board chairman

50 Years Ministry

80 Years Birth Day

MARCH 2017

From Ethiopia to India

In 2016, I visited an assembly in Scotland and mentioned in my report on Ethiopia that 50 years ago Sheena and I were ready to go to India, but our visas had been cancelled 12 days before we were due to sail and so we were not able to proceed to India.

At the end of the report, a young brother when he heard about our original exercise wondered if in the intervening years we had visited India. I told him that we had never travelled to India and that was the end of the conversation.

However, a week later I received a letter from the same young brother, and enclosed in the letter was the cost of the fare to go to India. I felt that I had to fulfil this exercise, and as a result I booked a flight to India to follow the end of my stay in Ethiopia in 2017.

Now it was not from 'India to Ethiopia' but from 'Ethiopia to India' as it was much cheaper to travel from Ethiopia to India than from London to India. I was there for 2 weeks. Originally I wondered how and with whom I would travel. For this trip I wanted to visit Mumbai and Sankeshwar and I felt that if I went with another brother who frequently visits India they might want to go to somewhere else.

In October 2016, I met an Indian brother called Barnabas who was visiting Northern Ireland for the first time, and he said that as he knew both places well he could arrange an itinerary for my visit.

I travelled to Mumbai and during my first week I stayed with Dr Stephen and Clare Alfred in Thane, which is a suburb of Mumbai. During that week I was able to see the work that Stephen is involved in at Bethany Hospital at Thane.

Dr Alfred is a general surgeon who had spent some time in the north of England, during which he met and married Clare who comes from Wylam.

Stephen was burdened to help his own country medically and so he returned to India and had a small hospital built. He found, however, that in the beginning things were a bit difficult. But there was soon such an interest that a new hospital had to be built in Thane and I was able to visit it during my stay there.

Hospital in Thane

The hospital sees around 600 outpatients daily. Stephen operates usually from 7am till 11am and then he goes and sees his outpatients six days a week. There is a wonderful spiritual ethos about the hospital and all over the place there are Gospel texts in English and Hindi. The hospital's motto is **'We come not to be served but to serve'**.

Beside the existing hospital there is a new one just being built to be used as a cardiac unit. This will increase the hospital's capabilities in helping the people in Mumbai.

There is also a dedicated band of believers who look after HIV patients. These patients mostly come from the poorer quarters of the city and I was able to spend some mornings with this group in the hospital and give them some words of encouragement. These believers visit the HIV patients in their own homes and are able to give help, material as well as spiritual.

The HIV team of believers

The assembly that the Alfreds attend originally met in a hall not too far from the hospital, but about three months ago the authorities told them that their hall was being demolished so that the road might be widened. But sadly there was no compensation offered.

At present the assembly meets in the basement of the hospital. I was able to be at one of their Gospel meetings and I noticed that there were patients from the hospital complete with their dressings etc. attending the meeting.

I visited another English-speaking assembly called Sharon and I had a very profitable time with them as well. I appreciated the splendid food in India which was very similar to the food in Ethiopia.

During my second week, I travelled by bus to a place called Pune where I was able to meet up with Barnabas who took me to his home for a lovely lunch before we travelled on to Sankeshwar. During my stop in Pune, I saw large numbers of motorcyles in this large town, the like of which I had never seen before. I was also able to see many Hero motorcycles which we had bought previously in Ethiopia.

Barnabas and I then travelled on to Sankeshwar and arrived there about 11pm. We were met by a brother who works in Sankeshwar. After 50 years, I had arrived in the very place where Sheena and I had originally intended to nurse in the leprosarium. The leprosy hospital ceased to operate in the 1970s, and the compound is now used for an old people's home with around 40 being well cared for.

In the morning Barnabas and I were invited to have breakfast with Miriam Keyse who is well into her 80s. She has been in India since 1964. Every morning in the hall on the compound they have a service for the residents and I really enjoyed the time with them.

Meeting at Sankeshwar old people's Home

I visited the village of Sankeshwar where there is a small cottage hospital. For some time the hospital has only been able to have had locum Doctors and its reputation has gone down, so not many patients have been attending.

However, recently two Doctors, a general surgeon and a gynaecologist, have come to the hospital and this may be the help that is needed. At the moment, they have very little income as there are so few patients, but there is quite a large expenditure. All are aware that this situation cannot continue as it is at the moment. The believers who run the hospital were asking for prayer about this situation.

Just opposite the hospital, there is a new building where the assembly meets. There is also a small hall adjacent to this new building which was the original hall. Barnabas and I spoke each evening in the new hall and a very good number of believers attended these meetings.

Old and new hall at Sankeshwar

On one of the days I travelled to Belgaum, the next town about 50 km from Sankeshwar. I was told that we were going to visit a planetarium in the afternoon. It turned out that this planetarium had been built by one of the evangelists to be used as an outreach in the Gospel.

The planetarium is of a very high standard. We saw the constellations, planets and stars and I was deeply impressed by the information that was being given. The evangelist told me that there are 52 planetariums in India - 51 are promoting evolution, only the one at Belgaum tells the story of creation. In the evening, I spoke at the assembly in Belgaum and on returning to Pune I spoke in their hall and then returned to Thane.

On my way back to Thane I was accompanied by four evangelists. In conversation, they explained that the political system was changing in India. For decades the party in power was mainly secular, but the new government is determined in the next few years to turn India back to being a Hindu nation. As a result the situation is becoming very difficult for the believers and the evangelists.

Christian Planetarium at Belgaum

Although it was just a short visit and I was able to see only a very small part of India, I felt that when the Lord closed the door to India and opened it to Ethiopia He had made the right decision for us. This can only be judged in retrospect, but I feel that what has developed in the last 25 years in Ethiopia in which we have been a very small part has all been guided by the Lord.

How true are the words in **Romans 11:33 - "O the depth of the riches both of the wisdom and knowledge of God! How unsearchable are his judgments, and his ways past finding out!"**

Hospital in Sankeshwar village

The author with four evangelists and Barnabas

CHAPTER TWENTY-TWO

Reflections

As I sit and contemplate these past 50 years, there are so many things I am so thankful about.

1. I am so grateful that both Sheena and I had godly parents who guided us in the right direction, although the final decision that we had to make was a personal one.

2. We thank God that while Sheena and I were in Ethiopia we kept remarkably healthy with no major problems.

3. We thank God for giving us a caring family who have been so supportive in all that we have sought to do for the Lord.

4. We thank God for the prayers, some known and others unknown, and for the practical support that we have experienced from the first day till the present.

5. I thank God for giving me such a loving wife and now that she has been called home to heaven I aim to continue to serve Him in Ethiopia and in the United Kingdom as long as I am physically able.

6. We thank God for living to see the day when from very small beginnings the work of God has grown beyond our wildest dreams.

7. We are convinced that this work has been a work of the Holy Spirit and it has been thrilling to see Him at work in the lives of people coming from Islam and Satan worship to Christ.

8. I am indebted to Fraser Munro for his meticulous checking of the final

draft of the book and for his helpful suggestions in regard to some of the sentences.

9. I am grateful over many years for the support I have received from *Echoes of Service* and *Interlink*, but I am particularly appreciative of the support I have received from the *Lord's Work Trust* who have helped me immensely in so many different ways.

10. We can only say in closing **To God be all the glory.**